# good food
## TO SHARE

SARA KATE GILLINGHAM-RYAN

PHOTOGRAPHY BY RAY KACHATORIAN

weldon**owen**

*Why do we gather to eat? We do it to nourish ourselves. But nourishment is much more than just fueling up to perform the day's tasks.*

The social interaction that surrounds a meal feeds the soul: we tell tales and seek advice, we laugh and cry, we learn and teach, and sometimes we even fall in love around chopping blocks and dinner tables. Because of that enticing mix, I see kitchens and dining rooms as sanctuaries not only of our physical health, but also of our general well-being.

A successful dinner party is one at which the guests feel relaxed from the moment they arrive. How do you achieve that? It calls for much more than knowing how to cook a steak properly, and it begins long before you answer the knock at the door.

Start with the ingredients: the best food is seasonally and locally sourced. The industrial food-supply chain has encouraged us to forget that behind every piece of fruit, cut of meat, and wedge of cheese lies a story. When people know where their food comes from, they feel comforted and empowered. Local, seasonal food also typically tastes better because it is fresher and because it is often grown with the health of both the consumer and the environment in mind.

I shiver at the thought that eating fresh, local food is regarded as "trendy." It should be second nature. But if you have not yet begun to eat this way, don't stress. Take the first simple step of supporting the food producers in your area whenever possible. They are nearly always raising the best-tasting and most healthful ingredients.

Studies that indicate that positive vibrations can move from the cook to the food he or she is preparing fascinate me, and although I'm not sure how the science behind such explorations works, the findings make sense to me. By cooking a meal for someone, you are sharing an intimate experience. You are pleasing their senses, but you are also sustaining their life. That's an honor! Take it seriously.

This book is intended to inspire convivial gatherings, but I hope that it also gives you ideas for making beautiful meals for yourself or your family on busy weeknights or lazy weekends. Only a handful of the recipes call for unusual ingredients or advance preparation, and every recipe was conceived with a festive, nourishing spirit. That spirit is something that you can summon to your table every day, whether the meal is a celebratory dinner party or a simple weeknight supper.

*Sara Kate Gillingham-Ryan*

## — MY PHILOSOPHY —

As a food writer, I have the pleasure of doing work that relates directly to my own survival. In other words, it's my job to cook and eat, and every meal is research. That means that the line between work and pleasure is blurred. Most people think of such proximity as a burden. But in my case, I feel lucky.

Even though working with food is what I do professionally, dinner parties in my house rarely allow much time for planning. Indeed, the decision to invite people over is more often than not made at the last minute. Sometimes just a prediction of snow is enough to get me on the phone inviting friends over for a cozy dinner. I'm fortunate to live in New York City, where just about any ingredient is within a ten-minute walk—geography that I'm especially thankful for when I've done little planning and folks are on their way.

I have a big basket on my bike, and I have been known to pull a granny cart around the neighborhood for large hauls. The vibrant Union Square Greenmarket is usually my first stop. Murray's, my favorite local cheese store, is around the corner from my apartment; a tiny butcher shop that blasts opera and has a sawdust-covered floor sits at the end of the same street; and across the way from my apartment is a bakery that turns out some of the best bread in the city. I realize not everyone is equally blessed, but I bet if you search, you'll find fresh food not too far away.

When planning a menu, I allow what's available locally and in season to guide me. This is how we should all be eating—not because it's hip, but because it's the savviest way to source our food and support our farmers. It takes a lot of resources to bring a spear of asparagus to your plate any time of the year except spring, so if you're not already following a local map and a seasonal calendar, you should give them both a try.

In the harvest months from May to November, a stroll down the lanes of the greenmarket inspires with produce of every color spilling onto the pavement. I just let the ingredients call out to me. In the dead of winter, the same lanes offer mostly apples, turnips, and a few greenhouse greens, along with the usual breads, fresh meats, and cheeses. But because our regional farmland is frozen solid for those dark months, I don't complain. Market vendors are eager to inspire a fatigued winter cook, so always talk to them. You'll find that they are a rich resource of culinary ideas. So, too, are fellow cooks. No matter where I'm shopping, I try to chat with people in line and behind the tables to find out what they are cooking.

Sometimes I'm buying for specific recipes that I'm testing for my writing projects. But just as often I return home with ingredients and no set plan, and they become pieces to a puzzle. Scores of solutions to the puzzle exist, and the more I cook—and believe me, I'm still learning—the more ideas I have. Beets can be prepared dozens of ways, a chicken can be cooked in countless styles, and a salad is a course with no rules. Let the ingredients—and a few good recipes, if you need them—guide you.

When I'm entertaining, I take the time to plan, but I don't get fussy. I avoid shortcuts like canned beans and tomato sauces, but I also try to enjoy the process and not get bogged down striving for perfection. I always leave a few small tasks for the guests to do; it's a pleasure to see people connect with their food. If there's not enough room in my tiny kitchen for the helpers, I send them to the living room with knives and cutting boards, and I make sure I put on some upbeat music and keep their glasses full.

If you have children in the house, get them involved in preparing food at an early age. Nothing gets people—young or old—more quickly interested in eating well than being a part of the kitchen crew. I've seen children's eyes widen with surprise when they slice into an heirloom tomato and discover the rainbow of colors inside. I've also seen adults marvel at tricks such as adding a pinch of salt to garlic as you mince it, to prevent it from sticking to the knife blade.

Unless the dinner is an impromptu attempt to try out a few recipes on friends when I'm on deadline, the ultimate goal of any dinner party I host is to connect people to their food and to share a meal together. That's it. I want to fill their bellies, of course, but mostly I want them to leave with a strong sense of connection to what they have eaten.

At the end of a meal, I am always happy if I have taught a guest something he or she didn't know. Even better is when someone teaches me something I didn't know, and that happens all the time. People, even those who don't cook much, usually have a tremendous store of food history. Many of my friends have detailed memories of older relatives who cooked the traditional dishes of their homeland. Other friends don't cook much but like to eat out, and they are happy to talk about memorable meals they've had on their travels around the city and the world. Still others know wine well and will guide a table of eight through an extemporaneous tasting.

These are the connections that make sharing a meal special. Of course, the food should taste good (a book full of wonderful recipes will help with that!), but what you really want to aim for is fostering a place, with your kitchen and dining table, where those connections will happen.

In an ideal world, the meal ends with some splatters on the tablecloth and a little dancing while we clear the dishes. If things have gotten messy and at least one person requests a recipe, I feel that I've put on a good dinner party and know that I've shared great food.

# Drinks

**Picking wine for meals** • White stone-fruit sangria • Watermelon mojito • Sparkling limoncello-raspberry cocktail • Cherry rum punch Sakerinha • Blood orange margarita • **Bubbly cocktails** • Michelada • Dark and stormy • Spiked watermelon agua fresca • Minty cantaloupe agua fresca Honey tangerine fizz • Fizzy blueberry lemonade • Iced minty yerba maté tea • Lemon verbena and mint tisane • Whipped hot chocolate

# — PICKING WINE FOR MEALS —

I didn't start drinking good wine until well into my twenties. By good wine I don't mean expensive wine. I mean wine chosen with care and curiosity. I had a few friends whose parents collected wine, which helped to whet my palate and made me realize that the wines I had been drinking were pretty terrible. I'm no sommelier, but I do know what I like and, armed with that knowledge, I can usually find a wine that will mate successfully with whatever I'm cooking.

**pairing pointers**  Balance is key. Either match or contrast the flavors of the dish so that the wine and food complement each other. Lighter dishes typically call for lighter wines, but characteristics of the food—such as saltiness, fattiness, bitterness, tartness, richness, or sweetness—should also influence your wine choice.

Salty foods go well with unoaked high-acid whites. With briny seafood, olives, or cured meats, pour an Albariño, a Txakoli from Basque country, a Greek Assyrtiko, a French Chablis, or sparklers like brut champagne or cava. With fatty, salty foods, such as a cheesy pasta, try a low-tannin, high-acid red, such as a Chianti, Bourgogne rouge, or Chinon.

Tart or high-acid dishes call for a wine of equal or higher acidity. For example, ceviche pairs nicely with a grassy, cool-climate Sauvignon Blanc such as Sancerre or a dry Riesling. For tomato-based dishes, fruity, high-acid Italian reds like Chianti, Barbera, or the spicier Primitivo work well, as do Greek reds from Nemea or Naoussa.

Fatty, rich dishes love tannic reds that cut through the fat and bind with the proteins. It's no surprise that a good steak likes a good Cabernet Sauvignon, Merlot, or Syrah. Aged and hard cheeses are also great with tannic reds. Most soft or creamy cheeses marry with whites.

With spicy foods, avoid high-alcohol wines, as they amplify heat. Anything off-dry works, however, because the residual sweetness and fruitiness of the wine allows the many flavors to shine through. German Riesling and demi-sec Vouvray are good choices. Dry rosés are another successful foil for spicy foods, because they are low in tannin but can be fruity, which complements the heat.

For sweet dishes or dessert, the wine should be equally sweet or sweeter. A classic combination is chocolate with Banyuls, port, or aged Malmsey Madeira. Fruit desserts are better with more aromatic wines, such as muscat and Sauternes.

## the rules

The best way to educate yourself about wine is to drink it. Find a great wine shop, ask questions, and then taste. When I find an affordable wine I like, I buy a case.

• Believe in your ability to choose a wine. In other words, trust your palate.

• There is no such thing as the perfect wine for a dish.

• How a dish is prepared (grilled, poached, fried, for instance) and its character (whether it's rich, light, or spicy) are often more important in determining the best pairing than simply by what the main ingredient is.

• Match the wine to the people. Ask yourself and your guests what they like. You'll also discover that talking about the wine is part of the fun.

I like a little bubble in my sangria, so I always add some sparkling wine. I also enjoy some kick, and that's where the triple sec comes in. Cool, light, and thirst quenching, white sangria is perfect for hot days. To maximize the "summer white" theme, use white peaches and nectarines.

# white stone-fruit sangria *serves 8–10*

2 peaches, halved, pitted, and cut into ½-inch (12-mm) dice

2 nectarines, halved, pitted, and cut into ½-inch (12-mm) dice

½ cup (4 fl oz/125 ml) triple sec

1 bottle (24 fl oz/750 ml) dry white wine, chilled

1 bottle (24 fl oz/750 ml) sparkling white wine, chilled

**add flavor**

If you have the time, marinate the fruit in the triple sec for a few hours to allow the flavors to mingle before adding the wines.

Put the peaches and nectarines in a large pitcher. Pour in the triple sec and still white wine and stir briefly to blend. (The mixture can be refrigerated for up to 3 hours before continuing.)

To serve, spoon the fruit-and-wine mixture into wineglasses or tumblers, filling each glass about half full. Top off each glass with the sparkling wine and serve.

# watermelon mojito *serves 1*

⅓ cup (1½ oz/45 g) diced seedless watermelon

5 fresh mint leaves, plus 1 small sprig for garnish

2 teaspoons sugar

2 lime wedges

Crushed ice

4–6 tablespoons (2–3 fl oz/60–90 ml) dark rum

Sparkling water

**fresh take**

I started sipping *mojitos* after a friend returned from a trip to Cuba hooked on the swoon-worthy national drink that combines mint, lime, and rum. A big crush of watermelon in the mix is not traditional, but in the summer when watermelons are crimson and bursting with flavor, it takes this potent cocktail over the top. I like dark rum in my *mojitos*, and I like them strong. This drink goes down easy, so if it's your first time, proceed with caution.

In a tall glass, combine the watermelon, mint leaves, sugar, and lime wedges. Using a cocktail muddler or the end of a wooden spoon, pulverize the ingredients in the bottom of the glass until the watermelon is a coarse purée, pressing on the solids to extract as much of the flavorful oils from the mint leaves and juice from the lime wedges as possible.

Add a handful of crushed ice and the rum. Top off with the sparkling water and stir gently. Garnish with the mint sprig and serve.

Someone once brought me a bottle of *limoncello* from Sicily, and it sat forgotten, collecting dust in a dark corner, for about a year. When I finally opened it, I found that the cheerful, bright yellow liqueur was imbued with all the lemon flavor one could ever want without any of the bitterness. So I started pouring it into fizzy drinks and mixing it with muddled fruits like crazy.

# sparkling limoncello-raspberry cocktail *serves 1*

½ teaspoon sugar

¼ teaspoon grated lemon zest

A few drops of fresh lemon juice

3 raspberries

2 tablespoons *limoncello*

Crushed ice

½ cup (4 fl oz/125 ml) sparkling wine

Lemon zest strip for garnish

On a small plate, stir together the sugar and grated lemon zest. Dip a clean finger in the lemon juice and moisten the rim of a champagne flute or other glass. Dip the rim in the sugar mixture to coat.

In a small bowl or ramekin, using a cocktail muddler or the end of a wooden spoon, pulverize the raspberries with the *limoncello.* Transfer the purée to the sugar-rimmed glass. Place a spoonful of crushed ice in the glass, then pour in the sparkling wine. Garnish with the lemon zest strip and serve.

**serve with**

This sunny drink speaks Italian, so embrace its homeland and serve with crostini, bruschette, or breadsticks. Or, set out a cheese plate with such Italian favorites as Taleggio or fontina.

# cherry rum punch *serves 1*

2 sweet cherries such as Bing or Rainier, pitted

1-inch (2.5-cm) chunk pineapple

1 teaspoon superfine sugar

¼ cup (2 fl oz/60 ml) light rum

¼ cup (2 fl oz/60 ml) fresh orange juice

2 tablespoons fresh lime juice

Dash of bitters

Crushed ice

In a cocktail shaker, combine the cherries, pineapple, and sugar. Using a cocktail muddler or the end of a wooden spoon, pulverize the ingredients in the bottom of the shaker. Add the rum, orange juice, lime juice, and bitters and cover and shake vigorously.

Fill a glass with crushed ice, strain the punch into the glass, and serve.

**fresh take**

A classic punch is always red. But not since I was ten years old and beat my Shirley Temple habit have I been keen on bright red grenadine, which is usually loaded with high-fructose corn syrup. So when it's cocktail hour, I look for alternatives to satisfy my nostalgia for a crimson punch. Here, I muddle fresh cherries to deliver both a rosy hue and a touch of sweetness.

Combining lime and spirits is always a win: a margarita does it with tequila, a gimlet does it with gin, and a *mojito* does it with rum. To put this theory to the test, I stirred together sake and lime juice for this spin on Brazil's national cocktail, the caipirinha. It's just as delicious, bright, and refreshing as all those other lime-and-spirits combos.

## sakerinha *serves 1*

1 lime, cut into 8 wedges

2 teaspoons superfine sugar, or to taste

Crushed ice

6 tablespoons (3 fl oz/90 ml) sake

Combine the lime wedges and sugar in an old-fashioned glass. Using a cocktail muddler or the end of a wooden spoon, pulverize the ingredients in the bottom of the glass, pressing to extract as much juice as possible from the lime wedges. Add a handful of crushed ice and top off with the sake. Stir and serve.

**fresh take**

Even though sake hails from another continent, I prefer its smooth flavor to that of *cachaça*, the usual base alcohol used for a traditional caipirinha.

## blood orange margarita *serves 4–6*

1 cup (8 fl oz/250 ml) fresh blood orange juice

¼ cup (2 fl oz/60 ml) fresh lime juice

1 cup (8 fl oz/250 ml) tequila

1 cup (8 fl oz/250 ml) triple sec

Coarse sea salt

4–6 thin blood orange slices

Crushed ice

In a pitcher, combine the orange juice, lime juice, tequila, and triple sec and stir to mix well. Spread salt in an even layer on a small plate. Moisten the rim of a glass with 1 of the orange slices, and dip the rim in the salt to coat lightly. Fill the glass with crushed ice, pour in the tequila mixture, and drop in an orange slice. Repeat to make the remaining drinks and serve.

**fresh take**

Blood oranges lend a unique, heady perfume and jewel red color to this classic cocktail. When they are out of season, Cara Cara oranges are a good alternative. The liberal pour I use here is a throwback to my twenties; you may prefer a version with less kick. Don't skimp when you are buying the tequila. Good-quality stuff is far superior and made with 100% pure agave. I like to serve these margaritas in jam jars loaded with crushed ice.

## — BUBBLY COCKTAILS —

Bubbles always make people feel festive. Even a glass of sparkling water perks up a dinner guest. Growing up, I thought champagne was only for weddings and New Year's eve toasts and for fancy people to drink with caviar. Then I got to college and someone introduced me to cheap cava in a black bottle that made me sick. Finally, a few years later, I learned the truth: sparkling wine can be affordable, doesn't have to give you a headache, and should be enjoyed on plain and fancy days.

Only wines made in the Champagne region of France are allowed to be called champagne. Other parts of France produce excellent, more affordable sparklers. Spain has *cava,* which is usually light and crisp. Italy has Prosecco (crisp and dry), Asti (sweet), and Lambrusco (two types, pink and semisweet and white and dry). The United States also produces a range of sparkling wines. I particularly like those bottled at Gruet Winery in New Mexico, where a French family makes them according to the Champagne method *(méthode champenoise).*

Sparkling wine pairs well with a wide range of foods, from buttery popcorn and nuts to cured meats and smoked salmon. Don't be afraid to serve it with a main course, especially if you've prepared seafood or a creamy, savory poultry dish. And if you walk into my kitchen when I am cooking dinner, you'll often find me with a glass of Prosecco in my hand, tasting my efforts with the help of some bubbles on the palate.

If the wine is a vintage year or in some way interesting, don't adulterate it. Otherwise, you can dress up a glass of bubbly, opting for a Bellini (1 part peach purée to 2 parts Prosecco or other dry sparkling wine) or a classic champagne cocktail (opposite). One of my favorite cocktails is even simpler: add 1 tablespoon Herb-Infused Simple Syrup (opposite) to a glass of sparkling wine.

## herb-infused simple syrup

½ cup (4 oz/125 g) sugar
½ cup (4 fl oz/125 ml) water
Herb of choice (see below)
*makes about ¾ cup (6 fl oz/180 ml)*

In a small saucepan, combine the sugar
and water, bring to a boil over high heat,
and stir until the sugar dissolves. Remove
from the heat, add the herb, and let stand
for 1–2 hours. Pour the syrup through
a fine-mesh sieve into a jar, pressing
down firmly on the herbs. Cap tightly
and refrigerate. The syrup will keep for
up to 2 weeks.

Herbs
3 fresh basil sprigs, 3 inches (7.5 cm) long
4–5 bay leaves
4–5 fresh geranium leaves
1½ teaspoons fresh lavender buds
¼ cup (¼ oz/7 g) fresh lovage leaves
2 fresh rosemary sprigs, 3 inches (7.5 cm) long
3 fresh thyme sprigs, 3 inches (7.5 cm) long

## classic champagne cocktail

1 rough-cut Demerara or other brown
sugar cube
¼ teaspoon angostura bitters
Cognac
Sparkling wine
1 orange zest strip
*serves 1*

Place the sugar cube in the bottom of
a Champagne flute or wineglass. Pour
the bitters on top. Add enough Cognac
to cover the sugar cube, then top with
the sparkling wine, leaving enough room
for the mixture to froth. Garnish with
the orange zest.

In Mexico, *micheladas* are crafted to cure a hangover. I think of it as a thirst-quenching cocktail for a lazy afternoon. Hops and carbonation blended with savory-sweet tomato juice produce a refreshingly spicy drink that goes down fast.

# michelada *serves 1*

1 tablespoon coarse sea salt

½ teaspoon ancho chile powder

1 lime wedge

2 tablespoons tomato juice

1 tablespoon fresh lime juice

1 tablespoon hot-pepper sauce

Ice cubes

1 bottle (12 fl oz/375 ml) Mexican beer, or to taste, chilled

### fresh take

Stateside, Tabasco may be the typical heat, but I like to use a Mexican hot sauce such as Cholula. Leave out the bottle and let people add as much as they like.

On a small plate, stir together the salt and chile powder. Moisten the rim of a tall glass with the lime wedge and dip the rim in the salt mixture to coat. Reserve the lime wedge.

Pour the tomato juice, lime juice, and hot-pepper sauce into the glass and stir to mix well. Fill the glass about two-thirds full with ice cubes. Gradually pour in the beer. Squeeze in the juice from the lime wedge and serve.

# dark and stormy *serves 1*

Crushed ice or ice cubes

¼ cup (2 fl oz/60 ml) dark rum

¾ cup (6 fl oz/180 ml) ginger beer

1 lime wedge

### local lore

A friend from Bermuda turned me onto these grown-up sodas. He says locals traditionally use Gosling's rum and Barritt's ginger beer. Other brands are fine, just be sure you use ginger beer, not ginger ale. This simple concoction combines the sweetness and spice of ginger, the tropical nuances of rum, and the citrus tang of lime in a rich flight of fancy that looks good, too.

Fill a highball glass with ice. Pour in the rum and then the ginger beer. Stir gently. Garnish with the lime wedge and serve.

All over Mexico you can find street vendors ladling out the brightly colored fruit drinks called *aguas frescas*. Although utterly simple, these lightly sweet mixtures of fresh fruit and water have knockout appeal and are the perfect choice for family gatherings. For grown-ups, I spike them with tequila, vodka, gin, or a liqueur to complement the fruit flavor, such as anisette with cantaloupe for an Italian flair.

# spiked watermelon agua fresca *serves 4–6*

4 cups (1¼ lb/625 g) cubed seedless very ripe watermelon

½ cup (4 fl oz/125 ml) fresh lime juice

⅓ cup (3 oz/90 g) sugar

1¼ cups (10 fl oz/310 ml) tequila

Crushed ice

Lime slices for garnish

Thin watermelon wedges for garnish

**double for a crowd**

Double the ingredient amounts for either *agua fresca* recipe and serve from a giant glass jar, just like you see on the streets of Mexico or in taquerias on both sides of the border.

In a blender, combine the cubed watermelon, lime juice, and sugar. Blend on high speed until the melon is completely liquefied and the mixture is smooth. Transfer to a pitcher and add 3 cups (24 fl oz/750 ml) water and the tequila. Stir to mix well.

Fill individual glasses with ice and pour in the *agua fresca*. Garnish each glass with a lime slice and a watermelon wedge and serve.

# minty cantaloupe agua fresca *serves 4–6*

4 cups (1½ lb/750 g) seeded and cubed cantaloupe, plus 12–18 small melon balls for garnish

⅓ cup (3 fl oz/80 ml) fresh lime juice

⅓ cup (3 oz/90 g) sugar

¼ cup (¼ oz/7 g) lightly packed fresh mint leaves, minced

1¼ cups (10 fl oz/310 ml) vodka

Crushed ice

Small mint sprigs for garnish

**go slow**

If you're using a liqueur, start with less to guard against an overly sweet drink. Use about ⅓ cup (3 fl oz/80 ml) first, then taste before adding more.

In a blender, combine the cubed cantaloupe, lime juice, sugar, and mint leaves. Blend on high speed until the melon is completely liquefied and the mixture is smooth. Transfer to a pitcher and add 3 cups (24 fl oz/750 ml) water and the vodka. Stir to mix well.

Fill individual glasses with ice and pour in the *agua fresca*. Garnish each glass with a skewer of 3 cantaloupe balls and a mint sprig and serve.

Sparkling-juice cocktails are the perfect solution when you need a festive drink for partygoers who don't want to drink alcohol. Also, when it is just too hot for wine or beer, these fizzy refreshers can be sipped all day long. For this fizz, I like to use the juice of Ojai Pixie tangerines, which are harvested in southern California in the spring and are distributed nationwide.

# honey tangerine fizz *serves 4–6*

3 cups (24 fl oz/750 ml) fresh tangerine juice

Juice of 1 lemon

¼ cup (3 oz/90 g) orange blossom honey

Crushed ice

2 cups (16 fl oz/500 ml) lemon- or raspberry-flavored sparkling water

Raspberries for garnish

In a large pitcher, combine the tangerine juice, lemon juice, and honey. Stir vigorously until the honey is completely dissolved. Add about 2 cups of ice, then slowly pour in the sparkling water. Stir gently.

Fill individual glasses with more ice and pour in the fizz. Garnish each drink with a raspberry or two and serve.

**fresh take**

During the winter months, make this fizz with satsuma mandarins or clementines.

# fizzy blueberry lemonade *serves 1*

Juice of 1 lemon

1 tablespoon honey

¼ cup (1 oz/30 g) blueberries

Crushed ice

Seltzer water

Fresh mint sprig for garnish

In a blender, combine the lemon juice, honey, and blueberries and blend to a smooth purée. Fill a glass with ice, pour in the blueberry purée, and top with a splash of seltzer. Garnish with the mint sprig and serve.

**ode to berry season**

Nothing gets me more excited about blueberries than a weekend in Maine at the height of their season. I pick the berries obsessively—"just one more handful!"—until the sun goes down. Compared to the hard labor (though rarefied rewards) of making jam or a pie, whipping up this berry-laced spritzer is easy and delivers nearly instant fresh-berry gratification. For an adults-only drink, trade out some of the seltzer for *limoncello* or vodka.

I first tried yerba maté when my palate was too young to appreciate its flavor. It tasted like tobacco to me, so I put down my glass until adulthood, when I tried it again and was quickly seduced by its bitter, pungent flavor. On hot days, I brew up a big jar of this tea, add honey and fresh-cut mint from my garden, and serve it in ice-packed glasses.

# iced minty yerba maté tea *serves 4–6*

1 cup (1 oz/30 g) lightly packed fresh mint leaves

4 yerba maté tea bags

3 tablespoons honey

Crushed ice

**fresh take**

If you are not a fan of the flavor of yerba maté, try making this tea with green tea, lemon verbena, or chamomile.

In a saucepan, bring 6 cups (48 fl oz/1.5 l) water to a boil over high heat. Remove from the heat. When the water stops bubbling, add the mint leaves and tea bags. Let steep for 5 minutes, then remove and discard the tea bags. Stir in the honey until dissolved. Let cool, cover, and refrigerate until well chilled. Pour over crushed ice in tall glasses and serve.

*See page 33 for photo*

# lemon verbena and mint tisane *serves 4–6*

1 handful fresh lemon verbena leaves and stems

1 handful fresh mint leaves and stems

Ice cubes or crushed ice (optional)

**fresh take**

Served either hot or over ice, a tisane (ti-ZAN) is an herbal infusion typically sipped at the end of a meal or for a pick-me-up any time of day. In the summer when my herb garden is flourishing, and especially when the plants shoot up tall spires that threaten to bolt and clobber other plants, I get out my pruners and snip the tops to make tisanes. Mix and match any herbs you like.

Place the herbs in a teapot of at least a 1-qt (1-l) capacity. Pour 4 cups (32 fl oz/1 l) water into a saucepan and heat to nearly boiling over high heat. (Boiling water will oversteep the herbs—that is, cook the delicate leaves to a point where they give off a grassy flavor that masks their true flavors.)

Remove the water from the heat, pour it into the teapot, and let the mixture steep for 3–5 minutes. Let cool slightly, then strain through a fine-mesh sieve into teacups or mugs and serve. Or, let cool to warm or room temperature and pour into glasses filled with ice and serve.

A cup of hot chocolate is a comforting end to a meal, and depending on the tone of your gathering or the menu itself, it can be delivered in the spirit of fun or as an elegant surprise. For the host, it may serve as the perfect easy finale, covering coffee and dessert in one sweet, steaming cup. Drop in a scoop of ice cream or a shot of brandy to make the treat even more decadent.

# whipped hot chocolate *serves 1*

½ cup (4 fl oz/125 ml) low-fat or whole milk

1 teaspoon unsweetened cocoa powder

1 teaspoon sugar

2 oz (60 g) bittersweet chocolate, finely chopped or grated

Pinch of salt

Pinch of ground cinnamon

Brandy for serving (optional)

Vanilla ice cream for serving (optional)

**serve with**

On a cold afternoon, I like to serve hot chocolate with a slightly savory snack, like slices of whole-wheat toast topped with European-style butter, tea biscuits, or shortbread.

In a small saucepan over medium heat, combine the milk, cocoa powder, and sugar. Whisk until the sugar dissolves and the mixture is warmed through. Add the chocolate, salt, and cinnamon and continue whisking vigorously until the mixture is frothy, smooth, and very warm.

Pour into a coffee cup or mug. Add the brandy or ice cream (or both!), if using, and serve.

# Starters

**How to build an antipasto platter** • Fruit with prosciutto • Classic deviled eggs • Caesar salad deviled eggs • Lamb meatballs in lettuce cups with minty yogurt • **How to build a cheese plate** • Smashed figs with walnuts and burrata • Marinated feta with olives and pita • **Crostini** • Cured fish platter with accompaniments • Crispy five-fragrance calamari and dipping sauce Spicy shrimp salad rolls • Beef tataki with vegetable slaw and ponzu • Hummus Muhammara • Bagna cauda with green beans • Herbed lemon-butter popcorn Maple-bacon spiced nuts

# — HOW TO BUILD AN ANTIPASTO PLATTER —

It was in Italy in the summer, in the walled Tuscan town of Lucca, that I first had really good antipasti. Deeply fragrant melon, perfect late-summer figs, freshly sliced sheets of *prosciutto di Parma,* and snowy white ribbons of supple *lardo.* It was a simple plate—just four elements—but the quality of the ingredients bowled me over.

Of course, place and mood influence taste memories, so it is impossible to re-create that Tuscan experience. But it is possible to get close. When I returned home, I figured out where in my neighborhood I could get high-quality cured meats for antipasti. At the time, it wasn't easy to find *lardo* (salt-and-spice-cured fatback and, yes, it tastes better than it sounds), but these days it is more widely available and one of my favorite additions to an antipasto platter. Ditto for *bresaola* (air-dried, salt-cured beef), which offers a stark textural (it is dense) and color (dark red) contrast to the *lardo.* This is one way to think about assembling a good antipasto assortment: a mix of colors and textures.

Another way is to think about the season. In the summer, I combine meats and fresh fruits. In the colder months, when the earth gives fewer fruits, I pair meats with preserved or cooked vegetables like cornichons, pickled beets, and roasted garlic, along with good-quality mustard and hunks of Parmesan.

To arrange a selection of antipasti, put little piles of bite-size morsels on a large platter. Of course, you can include anything you like—the word *antipasto* means "before the meal"—but if you're going for authenticity, chips and dip don't work. They also don't work because antipasti, unlike hors d'oeuvres, are eaten at the table, not while guests are milling around.

Among the possibilities are rustic hunks of cheese like Parmesan or *grana padano* or some lumps of fresh ricotta with a drizzle of olive oil. The classic pairing is prosciutto and melon (usually cantaloupe), but I also like prosciutto with stone fruits like apricots, plums, peaches, or nectarines, with a pinch of sea salt on the fruit. Figs go well with prosciutto and other cured meats, too. During citrus season, I combine thinly sliced *bresaola* and grapefruit segments. Including starkly white *lardo* is usually a plus, as it provides a stunning visual contrast to the usual deep colors of the other meats.

Opposite are some of my favorite elements for an antipasto platter, though I don't want you to limit yourself to what I suggest. Set out some coarse country bread or crostini to act as a landing place for spreads like pâté and for softer cheeses. And encourage guests to use their fingers when forks prove difficult.

## the components

I usually let the season and the occasion be my guide when composing an antipasto platter. Or, I just use what I have on hand—olives and meat from the fridge, nuts from the cupboard, baby carrots from the garden—and arrange the offerings on a platter. The key is mixing flavors and presenting a mélange of tasty tidbits that are easy to share. Here are a few of my favorite antipasti items.

**fruits and vegetables** sliced stone fruits sprinkled with flaky salt; citrus segments; melon wedges; figs; cornichons; pickled beets; roasted garlic cloves; braised fennel; olives

**cheeses** bite-size hunks of hard cheeses like Parmesan or *grana padano*; ricotta or fresh goat cheese with chopped herbs or fennel tops; *bocconcini* or torn pieces of fresh mozzarella; thin wedges of feta

**cured meats and seafood** prosciutto; *bresaola; lardo;* salami; *sopressata;* mortadella; liver pâté; *boquerones* (white anchovies cured in vinegar)

Melon is the fruit most traditionally paired with prosciutto, but this deep pink, delicate meat—the most prized of all Italian hams—is good with whatever summer fruit is in its prime. The fruit should be fragrant even before you cut it open, and the flesh should be firm, not mushy. A pinch of sea salt will bring out its natural sweetness.

# fruit with prosciutto *serves 4–6*

Nectarines, figs, cantaloupe, honeydew, and/or other ripe summer fruits

8 paper-thin slices prosciutto

½ lemon

Sea salt

Pit or seed the fruit, if necessary, and cut into halves or wedges. If using melon, cut the rind from the fruit. Arrange the fruit and prosciutto on a platter. Squeeze the lemon over the fruit, and then sprinkle with a pinch of salt.

Serve right away, instructing diners to wrap the fruit in the prosciutto.

**fresh take**

In the fall, I like to track down Fuyu persimmons, which taste of apricot and tomato and are one of my favorite fruits. In place of the prosciutto, I use northern Italian *bresaola*, a mildly sweet air-dried beef, or serrano ham.

When you are making hard-cooked eggs, you want to use eggs that are at least 5 days old, because superfresh eggs are difficult to peel. That means that if you're in the mood to devil, don't reach for eggs you've just bought at a farm stand or farmers' market. These are a favorite picnic classic that never go out of style.

# classic deviled eggs *serves 6–12*

6 large eggs, at room temperature

2 tablespoons mayonnaise

2 teaspoons Dijon mustard

1 teaspoon white wine vinegar

1 tablespoon drained and chopped capers or cornichon pickles, plus whole capers or chopped cornichons for garnish

1 tablespoon chopped fresh chives, plus more for garnish

1½ teaspoons chopped fresh tarragon

Sea salt and freshly ground pepper

### pack to go

I like to bring deviled eggs to a party or picnic—they are crowd-pleasers and easy to prepare—but I don't find them appealing if they've been assembled too far in advance. Here's my easy-to-transport solution: I hard-cook the eggs and make the filling ahead, then I store the whites and filling in two separate plastic storage bags. When I arrive at a party, I snip off the corner of the plastic bag holding the filling and pipe the filling into the whites.

Gently place the eggs in a saucepan and add tepid water to cover by about 2 inches (5 cm). Bring to a boil over high heat, then reduce the heat to low and simmer, uncovered, for 10 minutes. Using a slotted spoon, transfer the eggs to a colander and place under cold running water until cool.

Carefully peel the eggs and cut in half lengthwise. Remove the yolks and put them in a small bowl. Place the whites, cavity side up, on a clean work surface or plate.

Add the mayonnaise, mustard, and vinegar to the bowl with the yolks. Using a fork, mash and mix to form a paste. Stir in the chopped capers, chives, and tarragon. Season with salt and pepper. Spoon the yolk mixture back into the cavities of the egg whites, dividing it evenly and mounding it in the center. Alternatively, spoon the yolk mixture into a pastry bag fitted with a large plain or star tip and pipe the mixture into the whites.

Arrange the deviled eggs on a platter. Sprinkle with chives and more salt and pepper, dot with whole capers, and serve right away.

Here's my favorite variation on classic deviled eggs, an anchovy-laced tribute to Caesar salad. Be forewarned, they are highly addictive. For a light lunch, I'll serve these eggs with a plate of sliced garden-fresh tomatoes or a grain salad. They also make a great casual starter or finger food for a cocktail party.

# caesar salad deviled eggs *serves 6–12*

6 large eggs, at room temperature

2 tablespoons mayonnaise

1 teaspoon Dijon mustard

3 tablespoons chopped fresh flat-leaf parsley

Sea salt and freshly ground pepper

1 tablespoon olive oil

1 anchovy fillet, minced

1 small clove garlic, minced

½ teaspoon grated lemon zest

¼ cup (1 oz/30 g) *panko* bread crumbs

2 tablespoons freshly grated Parmesan cheese

12 small romaine lettuce leaves

## double for a crowd

When I make these eggs for a party, I usually double the recipe, because they always disappear fast. You can pipe the filling into the whites up to 4 hours ahead, and then cover the stuffed eggs lightly with plastic wrap and refrigerate them until about 15 minutes before serving. Then arrange them on the lettuce leaves, top them with bread-crumb mixture, and serve.

Place the eggs in a saucepan and add tepid water to cover by about 2 inches (5 cm). Bring to a boil over high heat, then reduce the heat to low and simmer, uncovered, for 10 minutes. Using a slotted spoon, transfer the eggs to a colander and place under cold running water until cool.

Carefully peel the eggs and cut in half lengthwise. Remove the yolks and put them in a small bowl. Place the whites, cavity side up, on a clean work surface or plate.

Add the mayonnaise, mustard, and 2 tablespoons of the parsley to the bowl with the yolks. Using a fork, mash and mix to form a paste. Season with salt and pepper. Set the filling aside.

In a small frying pan, heat the olive oil over medium heat. Add the anchovy and garlic and cook, stirring, until the anchovy begins to dissolve into the oil, about 1 minute. Add the lemon zest, bread crumbs, and Parmesan and stir to mix thoroughly. Continue to cook, stirring frequently, until the bread crumbs are golden, 2–3 minutes.

Spoon the yolk mixture back into the cavities of the egg whites, dividing it evenly and mounding it in the centers. Alternatively, spoon the yolk mixture into a pastry bag fitted with a large plain or star tip and pipe the mixture into the whites.

Arrange the lettuce leaves on a serving platter and place a deviled egg in each leaf. Sprinkle each egg half with about 1 teaspoon of the bread-crumb mixture, allowing some to spill down into the lettuce cup. Sprinkle with the remaining 1 tablespoon parsley. Serve right away.

I serve these small, allspice-flavored lamb meatballs, along with a dollop of yogurt-mint sauce, in little romaine lettuce cups, which makes them both eye-appealing and easy to pick up and eat. To find well-shaped, small leaves, look for hearts of romaine.

# lamb meatballs in lettuce cups with minty yogurt *serves 6*

½ cup (3 oz/90 g) bulgur wheat

Boiling water

½ cup (4 oz/125 g) plain yogurt

2 tablespoons chopped fresh mint, plus 2–3 tablespoons fresh mint leaves cut into narrow ribbons

1 lb (500 g) ground lamb

¼ cup (1½ oz/45 g) minced yellow onion

2 tablespoons chopped fresh flat-leaf parsley

3 cloves garlic, minced

⅛ teaspoon ground allspice

Sea salt and freshly ground pepper

2 tablespoons olive oil

12 small romaine lettuce leaves

1 cup (6 oz/185 g) cherry or grape tomatoes, halved crosswise

½ cup (2½ oz/75 g) seeded and chopped cucumber

### platter presentation

For a Mediterranean version of sliders, top crisp, salty pita chips with the meatballs and dollops of the herbed yogurt. If pomegranates are in season, tear one open to show off its garnet seeds (or, more properly, arils) and place in the center of the platter for a colorful centerpiece. Guests can also snag a seed or two, if they like.

Put the bulgur in a heatproof bowl and pour in boiling water to cover. Set aside to soften, about 15 minutes.

Meanwhile, in another bowl, combine the yogurt and chopped mint and stir to mix well. Set the yogurt sauce aside.

Drain the bulgur in a fine-mesh sieve and press on it with the back of a spoon to remove as much liquid as possible. Transfer the bulgur to a large bowl.

Add the lamb, onion, parsley, garlic, and allspice to the bulgur, season with salt and pepper, and stir to mix thoroughly. Divide the mixture into 12 equal portions and shape each portion between your palms into a ball.

In a large frying pan, heat the olive oil over medium-high heat. Add the meatballs and cook, turning as needed, until browned all over but still pink in the center, about 5 minutes total. Transfer the meatballs to a paper towel–lined plate to drain and cool slightly.

To serve, spoon about 2 teaspoons of the yogurt sauce into each romaine leaf. Top each with a meatball, 1 or 2 tomato halves, and 2 teaspoons of the cucumber. Arrange the filled leaves on a large platter. Scatter the mint ribbons over all and serve at once.

## — HOW TO BUILD A CHEESE PLATE —

When I moved down the street from one of New York's best cheese shops, my cheese consumption skyrocketed. Eating cheese more often has given me a slow and delicious education in the topic, but I still find the folks behind the counter at Murray's, my local haunt, to be my best teachers.

Talking with people who know their curds and then tasting firsthand is the best way to understand cheese. These days most cities and many small towns have good cheese shops or at least decent cheese sections in their local markets. One thing is for sure: people like cheese, so I almost always set some out for guests to enjoy just after they arrive, or I have a few pieces myself while making even the simplest weeknight meal.

**how to pick** My basic rule is to pick what looks good, and for that, you need to hit a well-stocked cheese counter where you can taste and ask questions. A good cheesemonger will help you build a great plate. If you want to take the lead, decide on a theme, such as texture. I often serve a soft cheese, a hard cheese, and something in between. Sometimes I opt to serve two to four cheeses from a particular country or region. You can be vague (French cheese) or specific (cheeses made by women in the northeastern United States). You can also highlight milk types, picking one cheese from each main category: cow, goat, and sheep. One of my favorite cheeses is *mozzarella di bufala,* made from the milk of the water buffalo. This luscious white pillow is divine on its own or carried on a baguette slice, wedged between tomatoes, or melted on pizza. The French cow's milk Époisses is a stinky cheese that I adore—and a real conversation starter. It is also, despite its heady smell, delicious.

**how much to buy** I generally plan on about 3 ounces (90 g) per person for an appetizer portion. Sure, some people will gulp down more than their share, but those guests are balanced by the ones who show restraint.

**how to accompany** I usually serve cheese with lightly toasted baguette slices. I also favor biscuit-like whole-wheat crackers. Spanish-style anise-speckled crackers are light, crisp, and ideal with goat cheese. I often put out dates, fresh fruit like grapes or figs, almonds, and/or olives. But the best way to eat most cheese is straight off your fingers.

**how to serve and store** Make sure the cheeses are at room temperature. Place them on a slab of marble, a wooden board, or a piece of slate or stone. Outfit each cheese with its own utensil, but don't fret about using knives that are specifically designed for certain kinds of cheese. To store cheese, wrap it in parchment or waxed paper and slip it into the refrigerator's crisper. Resist plastic wrap; cheese is alive and needs to breathe.

## cheese conversations

Learning about cheese, like wine, can sometimes be overwhelming. I've picked up a lot of information by talking with people—cheese lovers are a friendly lot. The conversations that break out among shoppers at my local cheese counter are veritable tutorials. I've gone in with a specific list and wound up taking home an entirely different selection because of recommendations from fellow customers. Once I convinced a gentleman to buy a wheel of Humboldt Fog when he overheard me ordering one and asked about it. I told him that I used to live in the area where it is made, and that the cheese maker knows her cheese. I'm sure he was pleased with his purchase.

When figs are in season, I can't think of anything I'd rather pair them with than a creamy cheese and caramelized nuts. Maybe it's because I learned about this combination from a dear friend, or maybe it's because the flavors of a rich cheese and a sweet, ripe fig are exceptional partners. Maybe it's both. I like the runny texture and bright flavor of *burrata*, a fresh Italian cheese with a center of thick cream encased in a supple shell of mozzarella.

# smashed figs with walnuts and burrata *serves 4–6*

for the caramelized walnuts
1 tablespoon honey
Pinch of sea salt
½ cup (2 oz/60 g) walnut halves

1 pt (8 oz/250 g) ripe figs, halved
or quartered lengthwise and lightly
smashed with the side of a chef's knife

1 ball *burrata* cheese, 8–10 oz (250–315 g)
Fruity extra-virgin olive oil
Flaky sea salt such as Maldon

Preheat the oven to 350°F (180°C).

To make the caramelized walnuts, in a small frying pan over medium-high heat, combine the honey, 1 tablespoon water, and the salt and stir to mix. Bring to a boil. Add the nuts and reduce the heat to medium-low. Cook, stirring constantly, until the liquid evaporates, about 2 minutes. Transfer the nuts to a plate and spread them in a single layer to cool. When cool, break up any clumps.

Spread the caramel-coated nuts in a single layer on a rimmed baking sheet. Bake until golden brown, 8–10 minutes. Remove from the oven and let cool.

Arrange the figs, cheese, and caramelized nuts on a platter. Drizzle some of the olive oil over the *burrata* and sprinkle with a little sea salt. Instruct diners to spread some of the cheese on a fig half, then top it with a caramelized walnut.

*See page 51 for photo*

### serve with

For a more substantial (and less messy) starter, I like to add slices of fruit-nut bread, torn pieces of crusty country bread, or firm, nutty crackers to the platter.

### fresh take

You can make this starter throughout the year by substituting whatever fruit is in season. When I can't find figs, I gravitate toward stone fruits, such as plums, apricots, peaches, or nectarines. I also like to garnish the platter with herbs clipped from my garden. Thyme, lemon thyme, marjoram, and basil are some of my favorites.

This savory combination of salty feta and briny olives, served with pita wedges, is a favorite easy starter. If I see a party date coming up on my calendar, I like to make a batch or two—or three—of marinated feta. Then, on party day, this simple hors d'oeuvre goes together in just minutes. I might serve up some hummus as well, and tumblers of rosé or Txakoli, a slightly sparkling dry white.

# marinated feta with olives and pita *serves 4–6*

½ lb (250 g) feta cheese, cut into bite-size cubes

4 fresh thyme sprigs

2 fresh rosemary sprigs

2 long orange or lemon zest strips

¼ teaspoon freshly ground black pepper

Pinch of red pepper flakes (optional)

1–2 cups (8–16 fl oz/250–500 ml) olive oil

4 pita breads, split

1½ cups (8 oz/250 g) mixed olives such as Kalamata, Niçoise, and Picholine

### add flavor

To add a little heat and spice to your olives, toss them with red pepper flakes, fennel and coriander seeds, and a little olive oil and marinate them for a few hours or up to 2 weeks. You can also vary the herbs you add to the feta; oregano, marjoram, or summer savory would be good.

In a large jar or other container with a tight-fitting lid, combine the feta, herb sprigs, zest strips, black pepper, and red pepper flakes, if using. Pour in enough olive oil to cover. Cover tightly and let marinate in the refrigerator to allow the flavors to develop, at least 1 hour or up to 3 days.

When you're almost ready to serve, preheat the oven to 350°F (180°C). Cut each pita half into 6 wedges. Arrange the wedges on a baking sheet and toast in the oven until warm, about 5 minutes.

Serve the feta in its marinade with the olives and warm pita wedges.

## — CROSTINI —

Crostini are slices of toast with a topping. The topping can be as effortless as a smear of pesto, or it can be more composed or seasonally driven. They are also a great way to use up leftovers, such as Short Ribs Braised in Balsamic (page 116) or Spring Vegetable Ragout (page 144). For a large dinner or cocktail party, set up a serve-yourself crostini station with warm toasts waiting under a dish towel and the fixings arranged on a platter.

## toppings

Here are some of my favorite toppings. Don't be stingy when you top the crostini, but don't overload them, either. You don't want to serve your guests a mouthful of toast. Nor do you want them to struggle to fit the crostini into their mouths.

**goat cheese, fig, and balsamic** A thick smear of fresh goat cheese, 1 or 2 equally thick fig slices, and a drizzle of reduced balsamic vinegar.

**wilted greens with lemon zest and sea salt** Kale and/or Swiss chard, wilted slowly on the stove top with stock or wine, topped with grated lemon zest and sea salt.

**white beans with red pepper flakes and oregano** Cooked white beans smashed with red pepper flakes and chopped fresh oregano.

**anchovy and pesto** An anchovy fillet topped with a substantial drizzle of pesto.

**herbed ricotta with olive oil and pepper** Fresh ricotta seasoned with chopped fresh basil, thyme, oregano, flat-leaf parsley, or sage topped with a drizzle of extra-virgin olive oil and a grind of pepper.

**roasted garlic cloves with basil olive oil and orange** A roasted garlic clove topped with a drizzle of basil-infused olive oil and a sprinkle of grated orange zest.

## classic crostini

1 baguette or ciabatta, cut into slices ½ inch (12 mm) thick
1 large clove garlic, halved lengthwise
Extra-virgin olive oil
*makes 30–40 crostini*

Grill or toast the bread slices. While they are still hot, rub them gently on one side with the cut sides of the garlic, then drizzle with a little olive oil. Finish with your favorite topping.

I'm a pushover for lox, cream cheese, and capers on rye. Here, that classic combo goes modern with crème fraîche and dark, rich smoked wild salmon. I usually tuck some vinegar-cured white anchovies—known as *boquerones* in the world of Spanish tapas—onto the plate, too, but if you prefer the oil-and-salt-cured anchovies native to the Caesar salad, use them instead. Don't be afraid to go light on the bread. The fish needs only a dab of crème fraîche to shine.

# cured fish platter with accompaniments *serves 4–6*

6 slices seedless rye bread

2 tablespoons unsalted butter, melted

¼ lb/125 g sliced smoked wild salmon

¼ lb/125 g cured white anchovies

¼ lb/125 g cured sardines

¼ cup (2 oz/60 g) capers, rinsed and drained

½ cup (4 oz/125 g) crème fraîche

1 lemon, cut into wedges

Preheat the oven to 350°F (180°C).

Cut each slice of bread in half on the diagonal. Arrange the halves on a rimmed baking sheet and brush the tops with the butter. Bake until golden, 10–12 minutes. Set aside to cool.

Arrange the salmon, anchovies, sardines, and toasted bread on a platter. Put the capers, crème fraîche, and lemon wedges in separate small bowls, or on the platter with the fish. Serve, inviting guests to assemble their own combinations.

**make it a meal**

I like to serve this cured fish platter as a light main course, with a cheese plate and a green salad, for a weeknight dinner with friends.

**serve with**

My go-to white wines are usually crisp, dry, and minerally. But when I'm serving cured fish, I pick a wine that has just a hint of sweetness, like dry Riesling, Gewürztraminer, or Pinot Blanc, or a sparkling wine such as Spanish *cava*.

Five-fragrance powder is also known as Chinese five-spice, five perfumes, or five heavenly spices. It is indeed heavenly: sweet, sour, bitter, and pungent, all in one blend. When I fry calamari, I add the spice to both the flour coating and the dipping sauce to double the flavor. Rice bran and grapeseed oil both have a high smoke point, making them ideal for deep-frying.

# crispy five-fragrance calamari and dipping sauce *serves 4–6*

for the dipping sauce

2 tablespoons Asian sesame oil

2 tablespoons honey

2 tablespoons chopped peanuts

1 tablespoon chopped fresh cilantro

1 tablespoon rice vinegar

1 tablespoon fish sauce

1 tablespoon fresh lime juice

2 teaspoons soy sauce

1 small shallot, coarsely chopped

¼ teaspoon five-fragrance powder (right)

1 lb (500 g) cleaned squid (tentacles and bodies), thawed if frozen

1 cup (8 fl oz/250 ml) buttermilk

¼ cup (1½ oz/45 g) white rice flour

1 tablespoon five-fragrance powder (right)

Sea salt

Rice bran or grapeseed oil for deep-frying

Lime or lemon halves for serving

## five-fragrance powder

It's easy to make your own five-fragrance powder. In a bowl, combine 4 teaspoons each ground cinnamon and freshly ground pepper, 2 teaspoons ground fennel, and 1 teaspoon each ground cloves and ginger. Stir them together, then store in an airtight container for up to 3 months. Makes ¼ cup (1 oz/30 g).

## platter presentation

This dish brings me to the beach, whether I am actually there or not, so I like to keep the presentation casual. I pile the calamari onto a board and serve the dipping sauce in a small bowl alongside. My guests can pick up the tasty morsels with their fingers and dunk them in the sauce—napkins optional.

To make the dipping sauce, in a blender or food processor, combine the sesame oil, honey, peanuts, cilantro, vinegar, fish sauce, lime juice, soy sauce, shallot, and five-fragrance powder and process until smooth. Taste and adjust the seasoning. Pour into a small serving bowl or individual bowls and set aside.

Rinse the squid and pat dry. Cut the bodies crosswise into rings about ⅓ inch (9 mm) wide. Leave the tentacles whole. In a large bowl, combine the squid and buttermilk and toss to coat well. In a shallow bowl, whisk together the rice flour, five-fragrance powder, and ½ teaspoon salt. Have ready a colander or medium-mesh sieve set atop another large bowl.

Pour the oil to a depth of 2–3 inches (5–7.5 cm) into a deep fryer or large, heavy pot, preferably cast iron, and heat to 370°F (188°C) on a deep-frying thermometer.

Working in batches, and using a slotted spoon, transfer the squid to the seasoned flour and toss to coat evenly, and then to the colander and shake off any excess flour. Still using the spoon, carefully lower the squid, a few pieces at a time, into the hot oil. Fry until golden brown and crisp, 1–2 minutes. Transfer to paper towels to drain and sprinkle with salt. Repeat with the remaining squid.

Serve at once, with the citrus wedges and dipping sauce.

One of my favorite Thai dishes is a minced meat salad called *larb*, usually chicken, beef, or duck marinated in lime juice and often quite spicy. Here's a lighter version made with shrimp, but it still has a dose of spice and tang from lemongrass, chile paste, and fish sauce. The mixture is wrapped in lettuce leaves with fresh herb sprigs—a tidy packet bursting with flavor.

# spicy shrimp salad rolls *serves 4–6*

1 lb (500 g) shrimp, peeled and deveined

4 tablespoons (2 fl oz/60 ml) fresh lime juice, or to taste

½ cup (½ oz/15 g) lightly packed fresh cilantro leaves, coarsely chopped

2 tablespoons fresh mint leaves, cut into thin ribbons

¼ cup (1 oz/30 g) thinly sliced green onion, white and tender green parts only

3 tablespoons fish sauce, or to taste

¾ teaspoon chile paste, or to taste

1 tablespoon peanut oil

½ red onion, very thinly sliced (about ½ cup/2 oz/60 g)

1 lemongrass stalk, tender midsection only, smashed with the side of a chef's knife and chopped or minced to yield about 2 tablespoons

4–6 large Bibb, butter, or romaine lettuce or napa cabbage leaves for serving

Small fresh mint and cilantro sprigs, shredded red cabbage, and shredded carrot for garnish

## dress it up

If you don't want your friends to do the work at the table, fill the lettuce leaves with all of the elements and then roll them up burrito style. Arrange the rolls, seam side down, on individual plates or on a platter lined with cabbage or lettuce leaves.

Chop the shrimp finely; the texture should be similar to that of ground meat. Place in a bowl and stir in 2 tablespoons of the lime juice. Marinate at room temperature for at least 5 minutes, but no longer than 15 minutes.

In another bowl, combine the cilantro, mint, green onions, the remaining 2 tablespoons lime juice, 1 tablespoon of the fish sauce, and the chile paste and stir to mix. Set aside.

In a heavy-bottomed frying pan or wok, heat the oil over medium-high heat. Add the shrimp and its marinade, the red onion, and the lemongrass and cook, stirring constantly, for about 1 minute. Add the remaining 2 tablespoons fish sauce and toss and stir until the shrimp is opaque throughout and almost all of the liquid in the pan has evaporated, about 5 minutes. Pour the reserved lime juice mixture over the shrimp and toss to coat evenly.

Transfer the shrimp mixture to a serving bowl and taste for seasoning. You may need to adjust the spiciness with chile paste, the saltiness with fish sauce, or the tartness with lime juice.

To serve, arrange the shrimp mixture, lettuce leaves, mint and cilantro sprigs, and shredded red cabbage and carrot on a serving board or tray. Instruct diners to pile some of the shrimp mixture on top of a lettuce leaf and top with sprigs of mint and cilantro and a large pinch each of shredded cabbage and carrot.

If I'm serving this appetizer with chopsticks, I like to drape the meat strips over the slaw, which makes it easier to grab a little of both. If I'm entertaining a group more comfortable using forks, I reverse the presentation and top the meat with the slaw. I serve the dish with my version of Japanese ponzu sauce, a light, bright citrus-based concoction that elevates the flavors.

# beef tataki with vegetable slaw and ponzu *serves 8–12*

1 beef tenderloin (about 1¼ lb/625 g)

2 teaspoons Asian sesame oil

Freshly ground pepper

¾ cup (6 fl oz/180 ml) soy sauce

3 tablespoons mirin (Japanese rice wine)

3 or 4 green onions, white and tender green parts only, thinly sliced (about 1 cup/3 oz/90 g)

2 cloves garlic, minced

1 tablespoon plus 1 teaspoon peeled and finely grated fresh ginger

¼ cup (2 fl oz/60 ml) fresh lime juice

3 tablespoons sake

1 tablespoon brown sugar

1 teaspoon grated lime zest

1 cup (5 oz/155 g) peeled and julienned daikon

1 large carrot, peeled and cut into julienne

1 cucumber, peeled, seeded, and cut into julienne

1 tablespoon black sesame seeds

## platter presentation

This dish looks beautiful on a long wooden board, such as those made for slicing baguettes. I mound the slaw in a pile along the length of the board, then drape the beef slices over the slaw. The result almost looks like sashimi.

Preheat the oven to 500°F (260°C). Rub the beef all over with the sesame oil, then sprinkle with pepper. Place on a rack on a rimmed baking sheet and roast until an instant-read thermometer registers 115°F (46°C), about 15 minutes. The meat should be very rare. Let rest for 10 minutes.

In a zippered plastic bag large enough to hold the beef, combine ½ cup (4 fl oz/125 ml) of the soy sauce, the mirin, half of the green onions, the garlic, and the 1 tablespoon ginger. Add the beef, seal closed, and marinate in the refrigerator for at least 4 hours or up to overnight, turning several times.

Remove the beef from the marinade and discard the marinade. Place the beef in the freezer for 15 minutes to firm it up for easier slicing. Meanwhile, make the sauce: In a small bowl, whisk together the remaining ¼ cup (2 fl oz/60 ml) soy sauce, the lime juice, sake, brown sugar, and lime zest. Cover and set aside at room temperature.

In a large bowl, combine the daikon, carrot, cucumber, the remaining green onions, the 1 teaspoon ginger, and the sesame seeds and toss to mix well. Remove the beef from the freezer and slice thinly on the diagonal against the grain. Lay the slices on a serving platter and drizzle with about one-third of the sauce. Add the remaining sauce to the slaw and toss to mix, then scatter the slaw over the meat. Or, pile the slaw on a platter and top with the meat. Serve right away.

I'm a serious dip addict. Some people can't keep their hands out of the cookie jar or the candy box. I can't keep mine away from a bowl of dip. While I won't deny using a spoon to snag a lick of hummus, if there's a salty chip, a wedge of pita, or a celery stick around, I'm the one loading it. A few bowls of flavorful dip and a generous bowl of dippers will keep folks tame until dinnertime.

## hummus  *makes about 3 cups (1½ lb/750 g)*

2 cups (12 oz/375 g) drained cooked or canned chickpeas

⅓ cup (3 fl oz/80 ml) fresh lemon juice, or as needed

¼ cup (2½ oz/75 g) tahini paste

¼ cup (2 fl oz/60 ml) plus 1 tablespoon extra-virgin olive oil

2 cloves garlic, finely chopped

Sea salt and freshly ground pepper

1 tablespoon chopped fresh flat-leaf parsley leaves

1 tablespoon pine nuts

1 teaspoon ground sumac or paprika

In a food processor or blender, combine the chickpeas, lemon juice, tahini, ¼ cup of the olive oil, the garlic, a big pinch of salt, and several grinds of pepper and process until smooth. If too thick, add a spoonful of water or lemon juice to achieve the desired consistency. Taste and adjust the seasoning. To serve, mound in a bowl and drizzle with the remaining 1 tablespoon olive oil and sprinkle with the parsley, pine nuts, and sumac.

## muhammara  *makes about 2½ cups (1¼ lb/625 g)*

3 large red bell peppers, about (2 lb/1 kg), roasted, peeled, and seeded or 1 jar (8 oz/250 g) roasted peppers

1 cup (4 oz/125 g) walnuts, toasted

⅔ cup (2½ oz/75 g) fine dried bread crumbs

1 small yellow onion, chopped

1 jalapeño or other hot chile, coarsely chopped, or 1 tablespoon red pepper flakes

2 cloves garlic, finely chopped

2 tablespoons pomegranate molasses

2 tablespoons extra-virgin olive oil

1 tablespoon fresh lemon juice

1 teaspoon ground cumin

Sea salt

8–10 fresh mint leaves, torn

In a food processor or blender, combine the peppers, nuts, bread crumbs, onion, chile, garlic, molasses, olive oil, lemon juice, cumin, and a pinch of salt and process just until combined. The mixture should have a coarse texture. Taste and adjust the seasoning, transfer to a bowl, and stir in the mint.

### dippers galore

Dippers are important players in the dip game, so choose them carefully. Fresh-cut vegetables can add pizzazz to the presentation, especially if you include a variety of colors, like orange, white, red, and purple carrots; a mixture of heirloom beans; or an array of radish varieties. Toasted thin baguette slices are a good neutral dipper, and warmed pita wedges dusted with salt or sumac pair well with Middle Eastern dips. And, of course, homemade tortilla chips surpass anything out of a bag.

*Bagna cauda* is a traditional northern Italian hot dip made with olive oil, butter, and anchovies. Don't say no to the combination until you have tried it, even if you think you don't like anchovies. The mixture clings deliciously to raw vegetables, forming an irresistible, rich, mildly salty coating. When young, tender green beans are in the market, this easy appetizer is a favorite.

# bagna cauda with green beans *serves 4*

3 tablespoons unsalted butter

3 tablespoons olive oil

3 large cloves garlic, crushed

6–8 anchovy fillets

⅛ teaspoon chili powder

1 tablespoon minced fresh flat-leaf parsley

Grated zest of ½ lemon

½ lb (250 g) green beans, trimmed

In a small saucepan, melt the butter with the olive oil over medium-low heat. When the mixture is hot (do not let it boil), add the garlic and remove from the heat. Add the anchovies to taste and stir, mashing them so they break up and begin to dissolve in the liquid. Add the chili powder, then place the pan over low heat and cook, stirring constantly, for 2 minutes, to allow the flavors to blend.

Remove from the heat and stir in the parsley and lemon zest. Serve at once with the green beans for dipping.

### fresh take

You can trade out the green beans for other dipping options. Some of my favorites are cooked shrimp, cooked quartered artichoke hearts, and raw or roasted cauliflower florets. Any leftover dip can be used to sauce chicken or fish, or drizzled over scrambled eggs on toast.

Hot, freshly popped popcorn can be dressed up dozens of ways to make it something special. In fact, it's hard for me to choose a flavoring: do I want it a little tangy, a little herby, a little sweet, a little salty? Here, a mix of lemon juice and zest, fresh thyme, maple syrup, and flaky sea salt covers all those cravings in one irresistible bowlful. Use a high-quality flaky sea salt, and substitute another herb, such as rosemary or parsley, for the thyme, if you like.

# herbed lemon-butter popcorn *serves 4–6*

4 tablespoons (2 oz/60 g) unsalted butter

1½ teaspoons finely chopped fresh thyme

1½ teaspoons fresh lemon juice

1 teaspoon pure maple syrup

1 teaspoon grated lemon zest

2 tablespoons olive oil

½ cup (3 oz/90 g) popcorn kernels

Flaky sea salt such as Maldon

In a small saucepan, melt the butter over medium heat. Add the thyme, lemon juice, maple syrup, and lemon zest and stir to mix well. Remove from the heat and cover to keep warm.

In a large, heavy-bottomed pot with a tight-fitting lid, heat the olive oil over medium-high heat. When the oil is shimmering, add the popcorn and immediately cover the pot. After the first kernels pop, cook, shaking occasionally, until all of the kernels have popped, about 4 minutes. Pour the popcorn into a large bowl.

Pour the warm flavored butter over the popcorn and toss to coat well. Season with salt and serve at once.

**dress it up**

A big bowl works just fine when serving popcorn for family movie night, but when hosting guests, I sometimes dress up this deliciously simple snack. Cut or tear newspaper, butcher paper, or parchment into square pieces, roll each square into a cone, and secure with tape. This allows guests, snack in hand, to move around during cocktail hour.

**fresh take**

Toss the buttered popcorn with freshly grated Parmesan or pecorino cheese.

As with most things we eat, the only way to make a bowl of bar nuts even better is to add fat and sugar. And if the fat comes from bacon, better goes right to best. For a party-worthy mix, splurge on high-quality bacon, and buy some fresh raw nuts: these staples of the snack drawer go rancid faster than you think. Use just one type—cashews get my vote—or any mix, such as hazelnuts and pistachios.

# maple-bacon spiced nuts *makes 2 cups (8 oz/250 g)*

2 cups (8 oz/250 g) mixed raw nuts

1 large egg white, lightly beaten

2 tablespoons firmly-packed dark brown sugar

1 tablespoon sea salt

½ teaspoon ground cumin

¼ teaspoon ground cinnamon

¼ teaspoon cayenne pepper, or to taste

¼ teaspoon ground ginger

4 slices bacon

1 tablespoon maple syrup

Preheat the oven to 350°F (180°C).

Put the nuts in a bowl and add the egg white. Toss to coat the nuts evenly.

In another bowl, stir together the brown sugar, salt, cumin, cinnamon, cayenne, and ginger. Add the spice mixture to the nuts and toss again to coat evenly.

Line a rimmed baking sheet with parchment paper. Scrape the nuts onto the prepared pan and spread in a single layer. Bake, stirring often to break up any clumps, until the nuts are lightly toasted, 15–20 minutes. Using a spatula, transfer the nuts to a plate and spread them in a single layer to cool. Leave the oven on and reserve the parchment-lined baking sheet.

Brush the bacon slices with the maple syrup and arrange in a single layer on the reserved baking sheet. Bake, turning once, until crisp on both sides, about 20 minutes total.

Transfer the bacon to paper towels to drain. Let cool, then break into small pieces. In a serving bowl, toss together the bacon and the toasted nuts, then serve.

## make it a meal

These bacon-studded nuts inspire me to turn a plain bowl of lettuce into a delicious main-course Cobb-like salad. I toss crisp romaine hearts with pieces of cooked chicken, avocado chunks, and a blue cheese dressing, then divide the salad among serving plates and garnish with the spiced nuts.

## serve with

I like to serve these spiced nuts on Thanksgiving day, putting them out for people to nibble on before the big meal. A light Pinot Noir from Oregon, with earthy, smoky notes, pairs well with this sweet and salty snack.

# Salads

Mostly herbs salad with three easy vinaigrettes • **Salad dressings** • Fresh corn, black bean, and tomato salad • Mexican chopped salad • **Chopped salads** • Crunchy salad with buttermilk-cumin dressing • Thai grilled beef salad • Fattoush salad Roasted beet salad with hazelnuts and roquefort • Bibb and mâche salad with oranges and olives • Roasted squash salad with dates and spicy pecans • Watercress and stone-fruit salad • Endive, radicchio, and apple salad • Summer tomato salad Winter greens with roasted pears and pecorino

This salad of tender microgreens and fresh herb leaves should be only lightly dressed. The herbs boast an enticing mix of flavors (if your thyme includes the blossoms, toss them in, too) and the microgreens—the youngest, smallest leaves—have an appealing texture and an intense delicacy. I have provided a trio of vinaigrettes to choose from. Each one is simple, balanced, and focused, all qualities that allow it to play the perfect supporting role to the starring salad.

# mostly herbs salad with three easy vinaigrettes *serves 4–6*

6 large handfuls mixed microgreens such as mâche, pea sprouts, and watercress

2 ribs celery, very thinly sliced

½ cup (½ oz/15 g) celery leaves

1 cup (1 oz/30 g) lightly packed mixed basil, fresh flat-leaf parsley, mint, chervil, and thyme leaves

for the lemon vinaigrette

2 tablespoons extra-virgin olive oil

1 tablespoon fresh lemon juice

Sea salt and freshly ground pepper

for the walnut-champagne vinaigrette

3 tablespoons walnut oil

2 tablespoons champagne vinegar

1 teaspoon finely minced shallot

Sea salt and freshly ground pepper

for the sesame vinaigrette

3 tablespoons Asian sesame oil

2 tablespoons fresh orange juice

1 teaspoon finely chopped fresh chives

Sea salt and freshly ground pepper

### serve with

This versatile salad belongs on the summer table. I serve it with grilled steak or seafood or with a platter of *bruschette*—slices of *grilled* bread rubbed with garlic, drizzled with olive oil, and topped with chopped tomatoes, basil, and sea salt.

Gently pat the microgreens dry on a clean kitchen towel. Pluck the leaves from the stems and discard the stems, along with any larger, tough leaves. Put the greens in a large salad bowl and add the celery and celery leaves.

Tear the basil into bite-size pieces and chop the parsley. Add all of the herbs to the bowl and toss to mix. Cover and refrigerate until ready to dress.

Choose a vinaigrette, then combine all of the ingredients except the salt and pepper in a small glass jar, cover tightly, and shake vigorously until well blended. Season with salt and pepper and shake again.

To serve, toss the greens with half of the vinaigrette. Taste and add more vinaigrette, if needed, and toss again. Serve right away.

## — SALAD DRESSINGS —

A dressing can brighten or tame a salad, depending on the flavors in the salad. A simple mix of greens, for example, does well with an equally simple oil and lemon or vinegar dressing. A dressing can also make the ingredients in a salad taste even better. The secret to a good dressing is to balance three elements: oil, acid, and seasonings.

Oils and other fats, like warm rendered bacon fat, balance the acid and add a soft sheen to the salad. Extra-virgin olive oil is the classic, but I also like using nut oils like walnut and hazelnut, Asian sesame oil (though I cut it with grapeseed or another neutral oil), and argan oil (pressed from the nut of a North African tree of the same name). I have two different olive oils in my pantry: one for cooking and one of finer quality for dressings. Always taste an oil first to make sure it isn't rancid. That happens more often than you might think, especially with nut oils.

Acids, which add brightness, include vinegars (balsamic in moderation and wine-based white, champagne, red, verjus, sherry, or rice) or citrus juice (lemon, lime, orange, or grapefruit). Soy sauce and rice vinegar are often the right match for Asian-inspired salads.

Seasonings add depth to the acid-fat foundation. Salt and freshly ground black pepper are the traditional additions, but there is no shortage of other possible flavors: a pinch of a fresh or dried herb, minced shallots or a teaspoon or two of Dijon mustard for body, a hot spice like cayenne, or a touch of sweetness from honey or maple syrup. I often add chopped capers or anchovies to a vinaigrette to build flavor.

**ratio** When cooks talk about salad dressings, they talk about ratio. The commonly accepted ratio for a vinaigrette is three parts oil to one part vinegar. I usually start with two parts oil to one part vinegar, however, and then begin tasting. The correct ratio depends on what ingredients you are using. Some oils are more acidic, some are more piquant. Some vinegars are softer, some are sweeter. You also need to consider the elements of the salad. For example, a salad with citrus segments calls for a less-acidic dressing. One with a creamy element, such as avocado or goat cheese, needs a brighter, more-acidic dressing to balance the fat in the salad.

**to shake or to whisk** In culinary school, I was taught to make dressing by adding the oil last in a painfully slow, steady stream while whisking vigorously. Now I generally toss all my dressing ingredients in a jar willy-nilly and shake it to whatever music is playing. You pick: I can tell you from experience that both work. For big batches, a blender is a time- and arm-saver.

## why homemade?

I always make homemade dressing because it takes just a few minutes and the taste is superior to anything you'll find on a store shelf. You can make a great dressing with as few as three ingredients that are probably already in your pantry. When dinner guests ask what they can do to help, I often suggest they make the salad dressing, a response that routinely makes them fret. But it is difficult to mess up the task because it includes just a few key elements, each of which is easy to adjust if the balance is off. I find that most salads are overdressed, but preferences vary widely, so I always make more than enough dressing. Dress the salad lightly (ingredients should barely glisten) and pass extra dressing for those who want more—or save it for tomorrow's salad.

## my go-to vinaigrette

2–3 tablespoons champagne
or sherry vinegar

1 tablespoon minced shallots

1 teaspoon chopped fresh thyme

⅓ cup (3 fl oz/80 ml) walnut, hazelnut, or other nut oil

¼ teaspoon sea salt

⅛ teaspoon freshly ground pepper

## my go-to creamy dressing

⅓ cup (3 fl oz/80 ml) extra-virgin olive oil

3 tablespoons white wine vinegar

3 tablespoons crème fraîche or sour cream

1 teaspoon Dijon mustard

*each makes about ½ cup (4 fl oz/125 ml), enough to dress a salad for 4–6*

Combine all the ingredients in a jar and shake well, or in a bowl and whisk well. Taste for fat-acid balance and flavor and adjust as needed. Add half the dressing to the salad, toss, and add more if needed to coat lightly.

This pretty, tricolored summertime salad goes Technicolor with the addition of bright green cilantro leaves and Mexico's snowy white *queso fresco*. I like to caramelize the onion to take off its sharp edge and to add a bit of sweetness, but if you want to skip cooking over a hot stove, slice the onion paper-thin and add the cayenne when you toss the salad.

# fresh corn, black bean, and tomato salad *serves 4–6*

1 tablespoon olive oil

½ red onion, thinly sliced

Sea salt and freshly ground black pepper

¼ teaspoon cayenne pepper

2 ears corn, husks and silks removed

1 can (15 oz/470 g) black beans, rinsed and drained

1 cup (6 oz/185 g) cherry or grape tomatoes, halved or quartered, or 1 large ripe tomato, cored and chopped

½ cup (½ oz/15 g) loosely packed fresh cilantro leaves, chopped

3 oz (90 g) *queso fresco*, crumbled

Lime wedges for serving

**serve with**

I put out a big bowl of this salad with a dish of homemade guacamole and a pitcher of *agua fresca*. When there's no time to whip up the *agua fresca*, ice-cold *cerveza* served with lime wedges makes a good stand-in.

In a heavy-bottomed sauté pan, heat the olive oil over medium-high heat until shimmering. Add the onion and stir to coat with the oil. Reduce the heat to medium-low, spread the onion evenly across the bottom of the pan and cook, stirring occasionally, until softened, about 10 minutes. Add a pinch of salt and the cayenne and cook, stirring occasionally, until the onion browns nicely, about 10 minutes longer. Remove from the heat and let cool.

Cut the kernels off the ears of corn. In a large salad bowl, combine the corn, black beans, tomatoes, cilantro, and cheese and toss to mix well. Season with salt and black pepper. Add the cooled onion and fold in gently. Serve right away with the lime wedges.

This salad is all about presentation. Chop the ingredients as finely or as coarsely as you like; just be sure to cut all of them into about the same size and shape. The results yield an eye-catching platter and requests for second helpings. Arrange the colorful ingredients in rows on top of the lettuces, and then appoint a guest at the table for the job of tossing.

# mexican chopped salad *serves 4–6*

1 ear corn, husk and silk removed

1 heart of romaine lettuce, cored and chopped (about 2 cups/4 oz/125 g)

1 small or ½ large head butter lettuce, cored and chopped (about 2 cups/2 oz/60 g)

1 cup (3 oz/90 g) diced red cabbage

1 cup (5 oz/155 g) peeled and diced jicama

1 large tomato, cored and diced

1 firm but ripe avocado, pitted, peeled, and diced

½ English cucumber, diced

⅓ cup (2 oz/60 g) finely diced red onion

¼ cup (2 fl oz/60 ml) fresh lime juice

1½ tablespoons honey

1 teaspoon *pasilla* chile powder

¼ cup (2 fl oz/60 ml) extra-virgin olive oil

Sea salt and freshly ground black pepper

½ cup (2 oz/60 g) roasted pumpkin seeds (*pepitas*)

⅓ cup (½ oz/15 g) chopped fresh cilantro

**fresh take**

If you're looking for flavor inspiration, take a trip to a specialty-food store, such as an Asian or Mexican market, or troll the international section of your favorite grocery store. Look for *pepitas* and *pasilla* chile powder in the Latin foods aisle.

Cut the kernels off the ear of corn and place in a small nonstick frying pan over medium heat. Toast lightly, stirring often, until the corn sweetens and the kernels turn golden around the edges, about 5 minutes. Remove from the heat and let cool.

In a bowl, combine the romaine and butter lettuces and cabbage and toss to combine. Spread the lettuce and cabbage on a platter and arrange the jicama, tomato, avocado, cucumber, corn, and onion in attractive rows on top.

In a small bowl, whisk together the lime juice, honey, and chile powder until smooth. While whisking constantly, add the oil in a slow, steady stream. Keep whisking until a smooth, emulsified dressing forms. Season with salt and black pepper.

Pour the dressing over the salad and toss to coat evenly. Sprinkle with the pumpkin seeds and cilantro and serve right away.

When I am in the mood for a one-bowl dinner, I often whip up a chopped salad. It's the perfect choice because it follows no rules: a mixture of chopped crunchy vegetables, sometimes tossed with lettuce and other chopped bits like cheese and meat. Nutritious, noisy, and easy to make, chopped salads are also great for clearing out the fridge or feeding a crowd.

My affection for the Cobb, the star of the chopped-salad universe, goes back many years to my first sighting of it on a restaurant menu that detailed its contents: hard-boiled eggs, avocado, bacon, and cheese. The moment I saw all those great ingredients in one place, I was hooked.

Nowadays, I like building chopped salads that are experiments in both taste and design. Sometimes they look like a bowlful of confetti and celebrate the season, such as a summertime mix of colorful tomatoes, yellow corn kernels, purple onion, and green cucumber or a wintry blend of fennel, beets, and squash. Other times, I keep all the ingredients a single color and vary the taste and texture.

*Nutritious, noisy, and easy to make, chopped salads are great for clearing out the fridge or feeding a crowd.*

All you need to make chopped salads is a bowl and a good sharp knife. But a mandoline is a handy addition to your tool kit. It can cut carrots and beets into matchsticks (julienne), slice an onion or fennel bulb wafer thin, and shred a head of romaine or cabbage with precision. Here are a few easy chopped salads to get you started.

**asian-inspired**  Shredded carrots, chopped green onions, shredded cabbage, and snow peas tossed with a dressing of Asian sesame oil, soy sauce, peeled and minced fresh ginger, and fresh lime juice and topped with toasted sesame seeds.

**monochromatic**  Anything green from the garden, such as green beans, fennel, romaine lettuce or purslane, and bell pepper, dressed with a pesto-infused vinaigrette and topped with chopped toasted pistachio nuts. Or go red, with chopped tomatoes, shredded raw beets, cubed steamed red-skinned potatoes, and thinly sliced red onion tossed with a red wine vinegar vinaigrette.

*panzanella*  Day-old coarse country bread cut into 1-inch (2.5-cm) cubes and chopped tomatoes, cucumbers, red onion, olives, basil, oregano, and flat-leaf parsley tossed with an anchovy-spiked lemon vinaigrette and topped with chopped capers.

Use an English cucumber for this salad. You don't have to peel it, plus the crunchy skin adds both texture and valuable nutrients. English cukes also have few, if any, seeds, so scraping them out goes quickly. Add the dressing slowly to hit the perfect amount: a sleek, light coating of herb-and-spice buttermilk.

# crunchy salad with **buttermilk-cumin dressing** *serves 4–6*

1 heart of romaine lettuce, cored and chopped (about 2 cups/4 oz/125 g)

3 ribs celery

1 English cucumber

4 radishes

2 tablespoons finely minced shallot

for the dressing
¼ cup (2 oz/60 g) crème fraîche or sour cream

¼ cup (2 fl oz/60 ml) buttermilk

1 teaspoon fresh lemon juice

3 fresh mint leaves, minced

1 anchovy fillet, chopped

½ teaspoon ground cumin

Sea salt and freshly ground pepper

**make ahead**

The chopped romaine and vegetables in this mix hold up well. Undressed, they will remain crisp in the refrigerator for up to 8 hours.

**dressing tip**

It's best to start with only about half of the dressing when tossing a chopped salad. Taste a mix of the ingredients and then add more if needed. Also, a chopped salad usually takes more dressing than a salad of delicate leafy greens does. Aim for a good balance of crunch and richness.

Place the chopped lettuce in a large bowl. Pinch off any leaves from the celery ribs and set aside. Cut the celery crosswise into pieces about ½ inch (12 mm) wide. Add the celery pieces and leaves to the bowl with the lettuce.

Cut the ends off the cucumber and cut it in half lengthwise. Scrape out any seeds with the tip of a spoon, then quarter each half lengthwise to make 8 long strips total. Cut the strips crosswise into pieces about ½ inch (12 mm) wide. Add to the bowl with the lettuce and celery.

Using a mandoline or a large, sharp chef's knife, slice the radishes into paper-thin coins. Add to the bowl. Toss together the lettuce, celery, cucumber, radishes, and shallot to mix well. Cover with a clean kitchen towel and refrigerate until ready to serve.

To make the dressing, in a small bowl or a blender, combine the crème fraîche, buttermilk, lemon juice, mint, anchovy, cumin, a pinch of salt, and a few grinds of pepper. Whisk or blend until smooth. Taste and adjust the seasoning. Refrigerate until well chilled, at least 10 minutes or up to 1 hour.

To serve, toss the salad with half of the dressing. Sample a lettuce leaf or two and a bite of vegetable. Add more dressing as needed to coat lightly and evenly. Serve right away. (Refrigerate the remaining dressing for another use. It will keep for up to 7 days.)

# thai grilled beef salad *serves 4–6*

### for the dressing

¼ cup (2 fl oz/60 ml) Asian sesame oil

2 cloves garlic, minced

1 teaspoon peeled and minced fresh ginger

2 tablespoons fresh lime juice

2 tablespoons fish sauce or soy sauce

2 teaspoons honey

¾ teaspoon chili sauce such as Sriracha, or to taste

½ lb (250 g) skirt steak

1 tablespoon peanut or rice bran oil

1 heart of romaine lettuce, cored and chopped (about 2 cups/4 oz/125 g)

½ medium cucumber

¼ red onion, very thinly sliced lengthwise

¼ cup (⅓ oz/10 g) each lightly packed chopped fresh mint, cilantro, and basil leaves

¼ cup (1¼ oz/40 g) chopped roasted peanuts

To make the dressing, in a small frying pan, warm the sesame oil over medium heat until glistening. Remove from the heat and add the garlic and ginger. Whisk in the lime juice, fish sauce, honey, and chili sauce. Pour into a medium bowl and set aside.

Preheat a charcoal or gas grill or grill pan over high heat. Pat the steak dry, then rub it all over with the oil. Place directly over the heat on the grill rack or place in the pan and cook, turning once, until nicely grill marked and done to your liking, 5–10 minutes total for medium-rare, depending on the thickness. Transfer to a carving board or a platter (you want to be sure to capture the juices) and let cool slightly.

When the steak is cool enough to handle, cut on the diagonal against the grain into strips about ½ inch (12 mm) wide, reserving the juices. Add the steak and its juices to the bowl with the dressing and toss to coat thoroughly. Cover and marinate at room temperature for 15 minutes or in the refrigerator for up to 12 hours.

Place the chopped lettuce in a large bowl.

Peel the cucumber and cut it in half lengthwise. Scrape out the seeds with the tip of a spoon, then quarter each seeded half lengthwise to make 8 long strips. Cut the strips crosswise into pieces about ½ inch (12 mm) wide. Add to the bowl with the lettuce. Add the onion and herbs and toss to mix.

Remove the beef from the dressing and set aside on a plate. Pour the dressing over the greens and toss to coat thoroughly.

Pile the greens attractively on a platter or divide among individual plates. Arrange the steak strips on top of the greens. Sprinkle with the peanuts and serve right away.

## fresh take

If you can find Thai basil, snag it for this salad. Its pleasantly pungent licorice flavor is unique and both contrasts with and complements the sweetness of the grilled beef. If you can't find it, sweet basil works just fine, too.

## pack to go

Because the beef is marinated in the dressing before it is combined with the lettuce and other fresh ingredients, this is a great salad to take on the road. Put it together at the party or picnic site just before serving.

Deep crimson ground sumac, the crushed dried berry of a bush widely found in the Middle East and the Mediterranean, is an essential ingredient in this dish. Its citrusy tang cannot be matched, so seek out the spice in Middle Eastern or specialty-food stores. Purslane, a sour, succulent Mediterranean herb, is also a classic addition, but if you cannot find it, use mâche or more romaine.

# fattoush salad *serves 6–8*

Olive oil for frying

1 large pita bread, torn into bite-size pieces

1 heart of romaine lettuce, cored and chopped (about 2 cups/4 oz/125 g)

1 cup (2 oz/60 g) purslane, chopped (see note)

1 cup (6 oz/185 g) cherry or grape tomatoes, halved lengthwise

1 cucumber, peeled, seeded, and diced

⅓ cup (1 oz/30 g) very thinly sliced red onion

3 tablespoons chopped fresh mint

2 tablespoons chopped fresh flat-leaf parsley

2 oz (60 g) *ricotta salata* cheese, coarsely grated (optional)

½ teaspoon ground sumac, plus more for garnish

for the dressing

3 tablespoons fresh lemon juice

½ teaspoon sea salt

¼ teaspoon freshly ground pepper

¼ teaspoon ground sumac

¼ cup (2 fl oz/60 ml) olive oil

**fresh take**

I think of *fattoush* as a Middle Eastern version of *panzanella,* Italy's popular bread salad. That's why I go the nontraditional route and add a handful of dry, salty *ricotta salata* to my version.

**make it a meal**

I like to turn this crunchy, flavorful salad into a light dinner by adding sliced grilled or poached chicken breast. For a crowd, I pile the salad on a platter, then top it with the chicken and pass a bowl of extra cheese at the table.

Pour olive oil to a depth of 1 inch (2.5 cm) into a large frying pan and heat over medium-high heat. When the oil is hot, add some of the pita pieces; be sure not to crowd the pan. Fry, turning once, until golden brown, about 1 minute. Transfer to paper towels to drain. Repeat with the remaining pita pieces. Let cool completely.

In a large salad bowl, combine the lettuce, purslane, tomatoes, cucumber, onion, mint, parsley, *ricotta salata* (if using), and sumac.

To make the dressing, in a small bowl, whisk together the lemon juice, salt, pepper, and sumac. Add the olive oil in a slow, steady stream, whisking constantly until a smooth, emulsified dressing forms.

Add the pita pieces to the salad and drizzle half of the dressing over the top. Toss to mix well. Sample a lettuce leaf or two and a bite of vegetable. Add more dressing to taste, if needed. (Refrigerate the remaining dressing for another use. It will keep for up to 7 days.) Sprinkle with a little more sumac and serve right away.

I love hazelnuts for their sweetness and Roquefort cheese for its earthy tang. But don't let my touting this classic combination prevent you from playing around with other possibilities to pair with the beets, such as pine nuts and crumbled *ricotta salata* or pistachios with shaved pecorino.

# roasted beet salad with hazelnuts and roquefort *serves 4–6*

3 medium beets, a mixture of red and golden, about 1 lb (500 g) total weight

¼ cup (1 oz/30 g) hazelnuts

2 oz (60 g) pancetta, cubed

Sea salt and freshly ground pepper

Large Bibb, butter, or romaine lettuce leaves

½ lemon

2 oz (60 g) Roquefort cheese, crumbled

1 tablespoon chopped fresh flat-leaf parsley

### fresh take

I used a mixture of golden and red beets here, but you can opt for one color only. You can also trade out the parsley for fresh oregano.

### easy dressing

The beets take a while to cook, but you save time on the dressing: it's just the fat left over from frying the pancetta plus a squeeze of lemon juice.

Preheat the oven to 450°F (230°C).

Trim the beets, removing the tops but leaving about 1 inch (2.5 cm) of the stem to prevent the beets from bleeding. Place the beets in a baking dish and tent loosely with aluminum foil. Roast until just fork-tender. Start checking at 30 minutes; it may take up to 1 hour, depending on the size and age of the beets.

While the beets are roasting, toast the hazelnuts and fry the pancetta. To toast the nuts, place in a small, dry frying pan over medium-low heat and cook, stirring constantly, until the nuts are fragrant and you can see they are just beginning to brown where the skins have flaked off, about 10 minutes. Remove from the heat and immediately pour the nuts onto a clean dish towel; they can burn quickly. Gather up the corners of the towel and rub the nuts together until most of the skins come off. (Don't worry about the bits that stick.) Chop the nuts coarsely and set aside.

Place the pancetta in a large dry frying pan over medium heat and sauté until crispy, about 15 minutes. Using a slotted spoon, transfer to paper towels to drain. Reserve the fat in the pan.

When the beets are fork-tender, remove them from the oven and let cool. When cool enough to handle, peel the beets by rubbing off the skins. To avoid staining your hands, use a paper towel. Cut the beets into slices or bite-size cubes, add them to the rendered fat in the reserved pan, and toss to coat. Season with salt and pepper.

To serve, arrange the lettuce leaves on a platter or on individual plates. Mound the beets on the lettuce leaves and squeeze the lemon over. Scatter the Roquefort, hazelnuts, and parsley over the top and serve right away.

*See page 87 for photo*

For many dishes, I like to use sun-dried olives because they have an intense flavor and are less acidic than brine-cured olives. Look for them online and in specialty-food stores; my favorites are from California. Their saltiness can vary, so taste carefully for balance before seasoning the dressing.

# bibb and mâche salad with oranges and olives *serves 4–6*

1 small head Bibb lettuce, cored and leaves torn (about 4 cups/4 oz/125 g)

½ lb (250 g) mâche, tough stems removed and separated into rosettes

1 fennel bulb, trimmed and cored, fronds reserved

½ small red onion

2 small navel oranges

½ cup (2½ oz/75 g) sun-dried black olives or other flavorful black olives

¼ cup (2 fl oz/60 ml) extra-virgin olive oil

Sea salt and freshly ground pepper

In a large bowl, combine the Bibb lettuce and mâche rosettes.

Using a mandoline or a large sharp chef's knife, slice the fennel bulb and the onion crosswise into paper-thin slices. Arrange the fennel and onion slices over the lettuces.

Using a sharp knife, cut a slice off the bottom and top of 1 orange to reveal the flesh. Stand the orange upright on a cutting board and slice off the peel in thick strips, following the contour of the fruit and removing all of the white pith. Hold the orange over a bowl and cut along both sides of each segment to free it from the membrane, letting the segments and any juices drop into the bowl as you work. Repeat to peel and segment the second orange. Strain the juice into a small bowl; you should have about ⅓ cup (3 fl oz/80 ml). Scatter the orange segments and olives over the fennel and onion.

Gradually whisk the olive oil into the orange juice in the bowl. Season with salt and pepper. Pour over the salad and toss to combine. Using scissors, snip about 2 tablespoons of the reserved fennel fronds and scatter over the top of the salad. Serve right away.

## fresh take

During the winter months, I incorporate citrus into salads at every opportunity. I usually rein in the greens and keep my focus on the citrus—blood oranges and grapefruits are favorites—mingling it with secondary ingredients, such as roasted pumpkin seeds *(pepitas)*, crumbled feta, or fennel. The licorice zip of the latter is the perfect foil for the tartness of the citrus.

## ingredient note

You can substitute other tender butterhead lettuces for the Bibb here, but it's worth seeking out the mâche. The clusters of spoon-shaped leaves are as pretty as they are delicious.

# roasted squash salad with dates and spicy pecans *serves 6–8*

Olive oil cooking spray

1 tablespoon sugar

Sea salt and freshly ground black pepper

4 tablespoons (3 oz/90 g) honey

⅛ teaspoon cayenne pepper, or to taste

¾ cup (3 oz/90 g) pecan halves

1 large acorn squash, 1½–2 lb (750 g–1 kg)

6 tablespoons (3 fl oz/90 ml) extra-virgin olive oil

¼ cup (2 fl oz/60 ml) champagne vinegar

1 tablespoon Dijon mustard

1 large head or 2 small heads curly endive, about 10 oz (315 g) total weight, cored, tough stems removed, and torn into bite-size pieces

¼ cup (4 oz/125 g) dates, pitted and quartered lengthwise

## make it a meal

This rich salad, composed of meaty, bright yellow squash, honey-and-spice pecans, sweet dates, and peppery curly endive makes a great side dish to roasted meats, pastas, or hearty soups. Or, serve it as a light main course accompanied with country bread and a cheese plate with perhaps a blue and a triple crème.

## fresh take

If you don't want to take the time to roast squash, you can substitute pears, apples, or Fuyu persimmons for an equally beautiful and flavorful salad.

Preheat the oven to 325°F (165°C). Line a rimmed baking sheet with parchment paper. Lightly coat the parchment with the cooking spray.

In a medium bowl, stir together the sugar and ¼ teaspoon salt. Set aside.

In a frying pan, warm 2 tablespoons of the honey over low heat. Add the cayenne and stir to mix well. Add the pecans and stir to coat. Spread the nuts in a single layer on the prepared baking sheet and toast in the oven until fragrant and lightly browned, about 10 minutes. Remove from the oven and let cool slightly, then add the nuts to the bowl with the sugar mixture and toss to coat. Discard the parchment paper and spread the pecans out in a single layer on the baking sheet to cool completely.

Raise the oven temperature to 450°F (230°C). Line a second rimmed baking sheet with parchment paper and coat generously with the cooking spray.

Cut the squash in half lengthwise and scrape out the seeds. Cut the flesh crosswise into slices 1 inch (2.5 cm) thick. Pile the squash on the prepared baking sheet. Drizzle with 2 tablespoons of the olive oil, season with salt and black pepper, and toss to coat. Spread the squash out in a single layer. Roast, turning several times, until fork-tender and lightly browned all over, about 25 minutes. Remove from the oven and cover with aluminum foil to keep warm.

In a bowl, whisk together the vinegar, mustard, and the remaining 2 tablespoons honey. Add the remaining 4 tablespoons (2 fl oz/60 ml) olive oil in a slow, steady stream, whisking constantly until a smooth, emulsified dressing forms. Season with salt and black pepper.

Put the endive in a large salad bowl. Pour in the dressing and toss to coat thoroughly. Add the warm squash, the pecans, and the dates and toss to combine. Serve right away.

This salad came into being on a rare cool July night, when cherries and nectarines were both in their prime but I wanted to serve something warming. Of course, you don't need to heat the dressing, but do give the fruit its quick sauté. That brief stint in a hot pan brings out its flavor.

# watercress and stone-fruit salad *serves 4–6*

¼ cup (1 oz/30 g) hazelnuts

6 tablespoons (3 fl oz/90 ml) extra-virgin olive oil

1 shallot, thinly sliced

1½ cups (9 oz/280 g) pitted and sliced stone fruit of choice such as plums, peaches, apricots, or cherries, or preferably a combination

3 tablespoons champagne vinegar or white wine vinegar

1 teaspoon Dijon mustard

Sea salt and freshly ground pepper

5 cups (5 oz/155 g) stemmed watercress, torn into bite-size sprigs

¼ cup (2 oz/60 g) crumbled *ricotta salata* cheese

**fresh take**

Here, the intense peppery flavor of watercress is the perfect foil for the fruit and warm vinaigrette. But when I'm in the mood for something more subtle, I opt for a milder green, such as spinach or frisée.

In a small, dry frying pan, toast the hazelnuts over medium-low heat, stirring constantly, until fragrant and you can see they are just beginning to brown where the skins have flaked off, about 10 minutes. Remove from the heat and immediately pour the nuts onto a clean dish towel; they can burn quickly. Gather up the corners of the towel and rub the nuts together until most of the skins come off. (Don't worry about the bits that stick.) Split the toasted nuts by applying pressure with your thumb and index finger until the halves separate. Set aside.

In a frying pan, heat 1 tablespoon of the olive oil over medium heat. Add the shallot and sauté until golden brown, about 7 minutes. Add the fruit and sauté for a few seconds, just enough to coat the pieces in the hot oil. Remove from the heat. Using a slotted spoon, transfer the fruit and shallot to a plate and set aside to cool.

Place the same pan over medium-low heat (do not wipe out the pan). Whisk in the vinegar, mustard, and a pinch of salt and a few grinds of pepper and cook, stirring, until the mixture bubbles and thickens slightly, about 5 minutes. Remove from the heat and whisk in the remaining 5 tablespoons (3 fl oz/80 ml) olive oil until smooth and emulsified. Taste and adjust the seasoning.

Put the watercress in a large salad bowl. Add the cooled fruit and shallot and pour the warm vinaigrette over the salad. Toss to mix and coat well. Sprinkle with the cheese and hazelnuts. Serve right away.

Crisp, pleasantly bitter Belgian endive and radicchio; matchstick-cut crunchy, tart apples (here's a good time to put Granny Smiths to work); crumbled salty bacon; and creamy ranch-style dressing—this salad has a flavor and texture to make every guest happy. The "greens" here are actually white and burgundy, so the apple is the only hit of green color in the salad bowl.

# endive, radicchio, and apple salad *serves 4-6*

3 slices bacon

½ cup (2 oz/60 g) walnuts

3 heads Belgian endive, cored and thinly sliced lengthwise or chopped

1 head radicchio, cored and chopped

2 Granny Smith or other tart green apples, cored and cut into julienne

½ cup (4 fl oz/125 ml) buttermilk

½ cup (2½ oz/75 g) crumbled blue cheese

1½ teaspoons fresh lemon juice

¼ teaspoon dry mustard

Sea salt and freshly ground pepper

### pack to go

Multiply this sturdy salad as much as you like and dress it on site.

### save for later

This creamy dressing is too good to go to waste. Any you don't use on the salad will keep in a tightly covered container in the refrigerator for up to 1 week.

In a frying pan, cook the bacon over medium heat until crisp, about 8 minutes. Transfer to paper towels to drain.

In a small, dry frying pan toast the walnuts over medium heat, stirring often, until fragrant and lightly browned, about 5 minutes. Immediately pour onto a plate to cool.

In a large salad bowl, combine the endive, radicchio, apples, and walnuts. Crumble in the bacon. Set aside.

In a blender, combine the buttermilk, cheese, lemon juice, mustard, ½ teaspoon salt, and a few grinds of pepper and process until smooth. Taste and adjust the seasoning.

Pour half of the dressing over the salad. Toss to mix well. Sample a leaf or two and add more dressing to taste, if needed. Serve right away.

When tomatoes are at their peak, I see no reason to do anything but serve them with the finest olive oil and sea salt I can get my hands on. I break this rule only when I crave *insalata caprese,* a traditional salad from Capri that pairs tomatoes; *mozzarella di bufala,* a pleasantly savory, addictively creamy buffalo's milk version of mozzarella; and garden-fresh basil. Splurge on heirloom tomatoes for this dish.

# summer tomato salad *serves 4–6*

2 lb (1 kg) ripe tomatoes, preferably heirloom, any shape and size

1 tablespoon table salt

Extra-virgin olive oil for drizzling

1 ball buffalo mozzarella cheese, about 7 oz (220 g)

1 handful mixed fresh sweet and purple basil leaves or sweet basil only, torn into large pieces

Flaky or coarse sea salt such as Maldon or *fleur de sel*

**serve with**

I like to serve this salad with grilled steak or fish, or, for a light meal, thick slabs of crusty country bread. Uncork a crisp white, a well-chilled rosé, or a light red to complement the menu.

Depending on the size and shape of the tomatoes, cut into halves, quarters, or uneven chunks to get pieces of roughly the same size. Place the tomatoes in a colander in the sink and sprinkle with the table salt. Toss well and set aside to drain for about 10 minutes.

Arrange the tomatoes on a serving platter. Drizzle generously with the olive oil. Using a soupspoon, carve out little pillows of cheese from the ball of mozzarella. Nestle the cheese pieces among the tomato pieces to make a pretty pattern. Scatter the basil on top and sprinkle with the sea salt. Serve right away.

I find that the kale, sorrel, and mizuna available at my local farmers' market make a good, pleasantly bitter mix to accompany the sweet roasted pear, but you can use any sturdy, cool-weather greens you like. If the greens are a bit tough, immerse them in salted boiling water for a few seconds, then dunk them in an ice bath to halt the cooking, or shred them finely.

# winter greens with roasted pears and pecorino *serves 4–6*

½ cup (2½ oz/75 g) pine nuts

1 firm but ripe Bosc pear, halved and cored

1 teaspoon olive oil

¼ teaspoon table salt

4 handfuls mixed winter greens (see note), tough stems removed and torn or cut into bite-size pieces

½ cup (2 oz/60 g) coarsely grated pecorino cheese

2 tablespoons champagne vinegar

½ teaspoon Dijon mustard

1 large shallot, finely chopped

¼ cup (2 fl oz/60 ml) nut oil such as walnut, almond, or pecan

Sea salt and freshly ground pepper

**double for a crowd**

This dish is a cinch to increase (just go a little light on the oil) and also holds up well. Serve it with roasted chicken, crunchy bread, and a carafe of red wine for a winter dinner party.

Preheat the oven to 375°F (190°C).

In a small, dry frying pan, toast the pine nuts over medium heat, stirring constantly, until fragrant and lightly browned, about 3 minutes. Remove from the heat and immediately pour onto a plate to cool; the nuts can burn quickly. Set aside.

Cut each pear half into 6 thin wedges. In a bowl, toss the pear wedges with the olive oil and the table salt. Arrange the pears in a single layer in a baking pan or on a rimmed baking sheet and roast for 5 minutes. Remove from the oven and, using tongs, gently turn the pears. Return to the oven and roast until tender and slightly browned, 3–5 minutes longer. Let cool.

In a shallow salad bowl, combine the greens, pine nuts, and cheese and toss to mix.

In a small bowl, whisk together the vinegar, mustard, and shallot. Add the nut oil in a slow, steady stream, whisking constantly until a smooth, emulsified dressing forms. Season with sea salt and pepper.

Pour the dressing over the salad and toss to coat thoroughly. Top with the roasted pear slices, season with a few grinds of pepper, and serve right away.

# Mains

Grilled cornish hens with chimichurri • Mediterranean-style slow-cooked chicken
Guinness-braised chicken • Brined pork loin with apricot-onion mostarda • Grilled steak
with charmoula • **My take on steak** • Cubano sandwiches with mojo sauce • Short ribs
braised in balsamic • **Slow cooking** • Fennel-roasted whole salmon • Cioppino with
toasted baguette • **Fish and shellfish for a crowd** • Sea bass poached with tomatoes
and pesto • Smoked-fish chowder • Black bean and beef chili • Basic pizza • **Pizza for
a crowd** • Spaghetti with five-herb pesto • Herbed spinach and emmentaler frittata
Chorizo and piquillo pepper frittata • White lasagna with mushrooms and prosciutto

# grilled cornish hens with chimichurri *serves 3-6*

for the *chimichurri*

1 cup (1 oz/30 g) lightly packed fresh cilantro leaves

1 cup (1 oz/30 g) lightly packed fresh flat-leaf parsley leaves

1 cup (8 fl oz/250 ml) extra-virgin olive oil

⅓ cup (3 fl oz/80 ml) fresh lemon juice

2 tablespoons grated lemon zest

2 tablespoons grated orange zest

4 cloves garlic, finely chopped

½ teaspoon sea salt

½ teaspoon red pepper flakes

¼ teaspoon ground cumin

3 Cornish hens, about 1 lb (500 g) each

3 tablespoons honey

olive oil for brushing

To make the *chimichurri,* combine the cilantro, parsley, extra-virgin olive oil, lemon juice, zest, garlic, salt, red pepper flakes, and cumin in a blender or food processor and process to a smooth purée. Cover and refrigerate.

To prepare the Cornish hens, first trim off and discard the extra fat from the necks and just inside the body cavities. Place 1 hen on a cutting board, breast side down. Using poultry shears, cut through the flesh and bone from the neck end to the tail along each side of the backbone. Remove the backbone completely. Turn the hen breast side up and spread it open. Cut out the breastbone and discard. Cut off the wing tips and any loose skin. Pull down on the legs to lay them flat. Turn the hen over and, using the palms of both hands, press down on the hen to flatten it as much as possible. Repeat with the remaining 2 hens.

Rub the hens all over with the honey and place them in a ceramic or glass baking dish or a large zippered plastic bag. Pour half of the *chimichurri* over the hens and turn to coat. Cover the dish or seal the bag and marinate the hens in the refrigerator for at least 1 hour or up to overnight, turning several times.

Prepare a medium-hot fire in a gas or charcoal grill. Separately wrap 3 bricks in heavy-duty aluminum foil. Brush the grill rack with oil. Remove the hens from the marinade and place, skin side down, on the rack. Discard the marinade. Position a brick on top of each hen so that it covers as much of the bird as possible. Grill until the skin is golden, 8–10 minutes.

Wearing oven mitts or grill gloves, remove the bricks. Using metal tongs and a large spatula, carefully turn over the hens. Replace the bricks and continue grilling until the hens are dark golden brown on the second side and cooked through, or until an instant-read thermometer inserted into a thigh away from the bone registers 165°F (74°C), 8–10 minutes longer.

If serving more than 3 people, cut the hens in half through the breast. Transfer the hens to a serving platter and brush with some of the reserved *chimichurri* sauce. Serve right away. Pour the remaining *chimichurri* into a small bowl and pass at the table.

## save time

It might not seem intuitive, but the technique of flattening poultry and cooking it under the pressure of a heavy brick saves time. It also produces impressive results: the birds cook quickly and evenly and acquire gorgeous color and crisp skin. If you're in a hurry, ask your butcher to prepare the birds as directed; this partial boning and flattening is also called spatchcocking.

## equipment note

You don't have three bricks lying around? Instead of bricks, you can use a pizza stone, cast-iron pans, or other heavy, flameproof pans to weight down the game hens while cooking.

This is one of my favorite ways to cook chicken. Basically, you dump everything into a big pot, and a few hours later, you have dinner. The idea of using bread crumbs comes from a Sicilian friend, who calls them the poor man's Parmesan. Here, I opted for *panko,* the Japanese version of bread crumbs, which are light and flavorful. The currants add a hint of sweetness.

# mediterranean slow-cooked chicken *serves 4*

1 large chicken, 3–4 lb (1.5–2 kg), cut into serving pieces

Sea salt and freshly ground black pepper

4 tablespoons (2 fl oz/60 ml) olive oil

1 yellow onion, chopped

5 cloves garlic, crushed

1 can (28 oz/875 g) plum tomatoes

1 cup (8 fl oz/250 ml) dry white wine

½ cup (2½ oz/75 g) pitted Mediterranean black olives such as Gaeta or Kalamata

¼ cup (⅓ oz/10 g) chopped fresh flat-leaf parsley

3 anchovy fillets, chopped

1 tablespoon chopped fresh oregano

2 bay leaves

½ teaspoon red pepper flakes, or to taste

⅔ cup (¾ oz/20 g) *panko* bread crumbs

¼ cup (2 oz/60 g) capers, rinsed and drained

2 tablespoons dried currants

Season the chicken pieces with salt and black pepper.

In a Dutch oven or other large, heavy-bottomed pot, heat 1 tablespoon of the olive oil over medium heat. Add the onion and sauté until golden, about 5 minutes. Add the garlic and sauté for 1 minute longer. Remove from the heat.

Arrange the chicken pieces on top of the onion mixture. Add the tomatoes with their juices, the wine, olives, parsley, anchovies, oregano, bay leaves, and red pepper flakes and nudge with a long-handled spoon to settle everything in the pot. Cover and return to medium heat. Bring to a simmer, then reduce the heat to low and cook until the chicken is extremely tender and starting to fall off the bone, 2–3 hours. Using a slotted spoon, transfer the chicken to a platter and tent with aluminum foil. Raise the heat to medium and simmer the sauce until thickened but still saucy, 10–15 minutes, breaking up any remaining whole tomatoes as it cooks.

Meanwhile, heat the remaining 3 tablespoons olive oil in a small frying pan over medium heat. Add the bread crumbs and cook, stirring constantly, until lightly golden, 2–3 minutes. Add the capers and currants and continue sautéing until the crumbs are deep golden brown, 5–7 minutes longer. Remove from the heat.

Distribute the chicken among individual plates or place on a serving platter, ladle the sauce over the chicken, and sprinkle with the bread crumb mixture. Serve right away.

### dress it up or down

I serve this dish in different ways depending on the occasion. For a casual Sunday dinner with family, I divide the chicken among wide, shallow individual bowls, ladle the tomato sauce over the top, and sprinkle with the bread crumb mixture (it's almost like a chicken stew). If I'm hosting company, I pile a bed of couscous on a serving platter, arrange the chicken over it, then top with a generous dousing of sauce and a sprinkling of the bread crumb mixture. I pour any remaining sauce into a small serving bowl and pass it at the table.

Until I visited Ireland, I had never thought much about the food my ancestors ate. What I discovered there was that although many Irish chefs were putting together imaginative contemporary menus, I was more taken with the traditional falling-off-the-bone-tender braised poultry and meat dishes cooked by regular folks around the island. I use Guinness stout here to boost the dish's Irish credentials.

# guinness-braised chicken *serves 4–6*

1 large chicken, about 4 lb (2 kg), cut into 6 pieces (2 breasts, 2 whole legs, 2 wings)

Sea salt and freshly ground pepper

2 or 3 yellow onions, about 1 lb (500 g) total weight, quartered

1 lb (500 g) new potatoes, scrubbed and cut into ½-inch (12-mm) chunks

1 lb (500 g) carrots, peeled and chopped

¼–½ small head green cabbage, cored and chopped (about 3 cups/9 oz/280 g)

5 cloves garlic, unpeeled

1 bottle (12 fl oz/375 ml) Guinness or other stout

¼ cup (2 oz/60 g) crème fraîche

Fresh chervil leaves for garnish

## equipment note

If you don't have a slow cooker, you can make this dish in a Dutch oven or other large, wide, heavy pot.

Pat the chicken pieces dry with paper towels and season generously with salt and pepper. Transfer the chicken to a slow cooker. Add the onions, potatoes, carrots, cabbage, and garlic and stir to combine. Pour in the stout and stir once or twice to settle everything in the cooker.

Cover and cook on low for 5 hours. Uncover the cooker and check one of the thickest chicken pieces; the meat should be cooked through and falling off the bone. If not, re-cover and continue cooking, checking again for doneness every 10 or 15 minutes.

Using a slotted spoon, transfer the chicken and vegetables to a platter, or divide among large, shallow individual bowls. Using a large spoon, skim any fat from the surface of the cooking liquid and discard. Squeeze the cooked garlic cloves from their skins into the cooker and stir until the garlic is mixed into the liquid. Spoon the liquid over the chicken. Put dollops of crème fraîche around the platter or on each serving. Scatter the chervil leaves on top and serve right away.

# brined pork loin with apricot-onion mostarda *serves 4–6*

½ cup (4 oz/125 g) kosher salt

½ cup (3½ oz/105 g) firmly packed brown sugar

1 tablespoon freshly ground pepper

1 yellow onion, finely chopped

5 cloves garlic, crushed

3 sprigs fresh thyme, plus 2 teaspoons chopped thyme

3 sprigs fresh rosemary, plus 2 teaspoons chopped rosemary

1 boneless center-cut pork loin, about 3 lb (1.5 kg), rolled and tied by the butcher

2 teaspoons olive oil

for the apricot-onion *mostarda*

1 tablespoon olive oil

1 yellow onion, thinly sliced

Pinch of kosher salt

¼ cup (4 oz/125 g) dried apricots (about 12), chopped

¼ cup (2 oz/60 g) sugar

¾ cup (6 fl oz/180 ml) dry white wine

2 tablespoons Dijon mustard

1 tablespoon white wine vinegar

### party pleaser

Cuts of pork of every kind are versatile, flavorful, simple to cook, and popular with a wide range of meat eaters. But pork is easy to overcook, and nobody likes dried-out meat. This loin, made tender and juicy with an overnight brine bath and served with a sweet and savory *mostarda,* will never let the cook down.

### make ahead

The *mostarda* will keep, tightly covered in the refrigerator, for up to 5 days. Reheat gently over low heat, with a splash of water to thin it, if needed.

### recipe redux

This recipe makes great sandwiches, which I discovered when I had leftovers after a dinner party. Smear a baguette with a little mayo or aioli and top with pork slices and a dollop of the *mostarda*—delicious! Enjoy with a glass of crisp, dry Riesling or a bottle of beer.

To make the brine, in a large saucepan, combine the salt, brown sugar, pepper, onion, garlic, and herb sprigs. Pour in 3 cups (24 fl oz/750 ml) water and place over medium heat. Stir until the salt and sugar dissolve. Pour 6 cups (48 fl oz/1.5 l) cold water into a large metal or glass container. Add the salt-sugar mixture and stir to combine. Let cool to room temperature.

Carefully submerge the pork loin in the brine, adding additional cold water if needed to cover the pork. Cover and refrigerate for at least 3 hours or preferably overnight, or up to 24 hours.

Preheat the oven to 350°F (180°C). Remove the pork from the brine and pat dry with paper towels (discard the brine). Rub all over with the olive oil. Sprinkle with the chopped herbs, pressing them into the meat so they adhere.

Place the pork in a roasting pan and roast for 30 minutes. Turn over the pork and continue roasting until an instant-read thermometer inserted into the thickest part registers 140°F (60°C), about 20 minutes longer.

Meanwhile, make the *mostarda:* In a nonreactive frying pan, heat the olive oil over medium heat. Add the onion and salt and cook, stirring often, until the onion has softened and is beginning to caramelize, about 10 minutes.

Add the apricots, sugar, wine, mustard, and vinegar and bring to a simmer. Reduce the heat to medium-low and simmer gently until the onion and apricots are tender and the sauce has thickened, about 10 minutes. The finished sauce should be thick but somewhat syrupy. Remove from the heat and cover to keep warm.

Turn the pork again and raise the oven temperature to 450°F (230°C). Roast until the top is browned, about 5 minutes longer. Transfer the pork to a cutting board, tent with aluminum foil, and let rest for 10–15 minutes. Cut into slices and serve with the *mostarda*.

*Charmoula,* a traditional North African sauce, contains a full palette of herbs and spices, from the green of cilantro to the red of paprika and cayenne to the gold of turmeric. I've been known to test the limits of this bright, heady paste by slathering it on roasted potatoes and omelets, or using it as a dip for warm pita wedges. Here, it is an exotic finish for simple grilled steaks.

# grilled steak with charmoula *serves 4–6*

for the *charmoula*

2 cups (2 oz/60 g) lightly packed fresh cilantro leaves and tender stems

1 cup (1 oz/30 g) lightly packed fresh flat-left parsley leaves and tender stems

⅓ cup (3 fl oz/80 ml) olive oil

2 tablespoons fresh lemon juice

4 cloves garlic, coarsely chopped

2 teaspoons peeled and grated fresh ginger

1 teaspoon smoked paprika

1 teaspoon ground cumin

½ teaspoon sea salt

¼ teaspoon ground turmeric

Pinch of cayenne pepper

Peanut or olive oil for brushing

1½–2 lb (750 g–1 kg) boneless rib-eye or strip steaks, at least 1¼ inches (3 cm) thick

To make the *charmoula,* in a blender or food processor, combine the cilantro, parsley, olive oil, lemon juice, garlic, ginger, paprika, cumin, salt, turmeric, and cayenne pepper. Process until the herbs are finely chopped and the sauce is well blended, stopping the machine and scraping down the sides of the jar or work bowl as needed. (Or, combine in a mortar and pulverize with a pestle.) Taste and adjust the seasoning. Set aside at room temperature until ready to serve.

Prepare a hot fire in a charcoal grill or preheat a gas grill to high. Brush the grill rack with peanut oil. Pat the steaks dry and arrange directly over the heat on the grill. Sear for 1–2 minutes on the first side, then turn and sear for 1–2 minutes on the second side. Take care not to let the flames flare up; if they do, move the steaks to the side until the flare-up subsides, then return to direct heat.

After the steaks have cooked for 4–6 minutes total, turn them again and move them to the cooler edge of the grill. Cover the grill and let cook to the desired doneness, about 3 minutes longer for medium-rare; an instant-read meat thermometer inserted into the thickest part of a steak should register 125°F (52°C).

Transfer the steaks to a cutting board. Tent with aluminum foil and let rest for 10 minutes.

To serve, pour the *charmoula* into a small bowl. Cut the steaks against the grain on the diagonal into thin slices and arrange on a serving platter along with the *charmoula.* Serve right away.

## change the method

If I don't feel like grilling, I pan-roast steak. It is easy to do: Preheat the oven to 400°F (200°C). Place a cast-iron or other ovenproof frying pan large enough to hold the steaks in a single layer without crowding on the stove top over high heat. When the pan begins to smoke, arrange the steaks in the pan and sear for 1 minute on each side. Transfer the pan to the oven and roast until browned on the bottom, about 5 minutes. Remove from the oven and turn the steaks. Return to the oven and cook to the desired doneness, about 3 minutes longer for medium-rare.

## make ahead

You can make the *charmoula* up to 3 days ahead of time. Pour a thin layer of olive oil on top, cover tightly, and refrigerate. Bring to room temperature before serving.

## — MY TAKE ON STEAK —

Whether I am serving steak or fixing a lower-priced cut of beef, I always spring for grass-fed, hormone-free meat because it's better for the land, the farmer, and you. Don't be afraid to ask your butcher where the meat in his or her case comes from and how it is raised. When steak is on the menu, rib eye and porterhouse are the two cuts I splurge on. Skirt and hanger steak are relatively lean options, but they still have a respectable amount of marbling and thus flavor. A hanger steak usually runs half the price of a rib eye. Flank steaks are long, flat pieces that can be thinly sliced for fajitas or for drying in the oven for jerky.

**my guiding principles for meat** Folks can debate the issue of the morality of killing animals until laryngitis halts the discussion and still not agree. That said, most people concede that good reasons exist not to eat meat. I think there are also a few great reasons to eat meat.

Except for a brief flirtation in high school with vegetarianism, I have always been a meat eater, and I have carefully considered the morality of that decision. I believe in the notion that we cannot thrive without killing something. Each plant we rip from the earth disrupts the life of many insects. Where's the line? Some people argue that we shouldn't eat meat because of the way most of it is raised, but I would rather support the many farmers who are trying to do the right thing by raising grass-fed beef without growth hormones and with few, if any, antibiotics and by treating their herds well in both life and death. Also, I feel more energetic and strong when I'm eating meat a few times a week. And finally, I get a lot of pleasure out of cooking and eating meat—good meat, that is.

Bad meat is raised irresponsibly, butchered poorly, cooked badly, or all of the above. That's what makes it cheap. Good meat costs more money. So, eat less of it and honor the animal that gave its life for your dinner by learning to cook it well.

**a good pan sauce** If you've cooked your steak in a pan on the stove top or in the oven, a splash of wine, water, or stock and a small knob of butter will help dislodge any precious bits of burnt meat and caramelized sugars on the bottom of the pan to make a sauce. Go easy on the liquid; you don't want to dilute the pan drippings too much, so start with a tablespoon or two, then taste for seasoning. Depending on what you did to the meat before cooking it, you may need salt, pepper, herbs, or finely chopped shallots (sauté the latter in the butter and pan bits before adding the liquid) to give the sauce some oomph. Then, if you like, finish the sauce by whisking in a few cubes of cold butter for a thicker body and a nice sheen.

## cook the perfect steak

Every cook has their formula for achieving a perfectly cooked steak and they vary quite a bit. My own method came together after watching and learning from some experts, practicing, and patching together this set of rules. Trust me, I've done plenty of experimenting.

1  Salt both sides of the steak with kosher salt—a dusting, not a dumping—and bring the steak to room temperature before cooking.

2  Blot away the moisture, then give the steak a quick olive-oil massage.

3  Get the cooking surface—grill rack or cast-iron pan—superhot before you add the steak.

4  Coat the cooking surface with oil that has a high smoke point, such as peanut oil, rubbing it on the grill rack or adding a spoonful to the pan.

5  Sear the steak on both sides—barely a minute per side is all that's needed.

6  Move the seared steak to the cooler side of the grill or transfer the pan to a 400°F (200°C) oven. Depending on the cut, the finishing stage will take as little as 1 minute or as long as 10 minutes.

7  Test for doneness with an instant-read thermometer, inserting it horizontally into the center of the steak without touching bone. I take my steaks off at 125°F (52°C) for barely medium-rare or 140°F (60°C) for medium. If you want well-done meat, you can cook it to 150°F (65°C) or more, but don't complain to me that it doesn't taste good!

8  Tent the steak with aluminum foil and let it rest for 5 to 10 minutes before serving.

# cubano sandwiches with mojo sauce *serves 8–12*

for the *mojo* sauce
½ cup (4 fl oz/125 ml) fresh orange juice
¼ cup (2 fl oz/60 ml) fresh lime juice
½ cup (½ oz/15 g) fresh cilantro leaves
3 cloves garlic, chopped
1½ teaspoons grated orange zest
1½ teaspoons dried oregano
1½ teaspoons ground cumin
Sea salt and freshly ground pepper
1 cup (8 fl oz/250 ml) olive oil

1 pork tenderloin (about 1 lb/500 g)
Salt and freshly ground pepper
1 tablespoon olive oil
2 ciabatta or other rustic loaves, each about 11 by 6 inches (28 by 15 cm)
½ cup (4 oz/120 g) sweet-hot mustard or honey mustard
½ lb (250 g) thinly sliced ham
½ lb (250 g) thinly sliced Swiss cheese
⅔ cup (4 oz/125 g) chopped dill pickles

## my own spin

*Cubanos* are traditionally sandwiched in a soft, sweet bread found at Cuban bakeries and then cooked in a customized sandwich press. For an easy crowd-pleaser, I split large ciabatta loaves, layer the ingredients, flatten the sandwiches with my hands, and bake them wrapped in foil. I make up for the missing sweetness found in Cuban bread by spreading the ciabatta with sweet-hot or honey mustard.

## make ahead

You can let the pork cool to room temperature, wrap tightly, and refrigerate for up to 3 days. The *mojo* sauce can be made up to 3 days ahead and stored tightly covered in the refrigerator.

To make the *mojo* sauce, in a blender or food processor, combine the orange juice, lime juice, cilantro, garlic, orange zest, oregano, cumin, 1 teaspoon salt, and 1 teaspoon pepper and process to combine. With the machine running, add the olive oil in a slow, steady stream and process until a smooth, emulsified sauce forms.

Rub the tenderloin all over with salt and pepper and place in a glass baking dish or zippered plastic bag. Pour in ¾ cup (6 fl oz/180 ml) of the sauce and turn the pork to coat on all sides. Let marinate in the refrigerator for at least 2 hours or up to overnight. Cover the remaining sauce and refrigerate until ready to use.

Preheat the oven to 500°F (260°C). Remove the pork from the marinade (discard the marinade) and pat lightly with paper towels. Heat a large cast-iron or other heavy ovenproof frying pan over medium-high heat and add the olive oil. When the oil is hot, add the pork and sear, turning as needed, until browned on all sides, 1–2 minutes total. Transfer the pan to the oven and roast until an instant-read thermometer inserted into the thickest part registers 155°F (68°C), about 5 minutes. Transfer the pork to a plate, tent loosely with aluminum foil, and let rest for about 10 minutes. Reduce the oven temperature to 400°F (200°C).

To assemble the sandwiches, split the loaves in half lengthwise. Spread the cut side of half of each loaf with ¼ cup (2 oz/60 g) of the mustard. Brush the cut side of the other halves with the *mojo* sauce. Cut the pork against the grain on the diagonal into thin slices. Lightly brushing each pork slice with *mojo* sauce as you go, layer the pork slices evenly across the bottom halves of both loaves. Top each with half of the ham, then half of the cheese. Scatter the pickles over the cheese. Replace the tops. Press each sandwich to flatten it as much as possible, then wrap tightly in aluminum foil, positioning the seam on top of the package. Bake for 5 minutes. Unwrap the foil just to expose the sandwich tops and continue baking just until the tops are crisp, about 2 minutes longer. Transfer the packages to a cutting board and let the loaves rest in the foil for about 10 minutes. Unwrap completely and, using a long serrated knife, cut each loaf crosswise into pieces and serve right away.

Many cooks—and eaters—think of braised short ribs, country bread, and a big red wine as the perfect winter menu. But these fork-tender short ribs make a great summer dish, too. You can braise them in a slow cooker and then serve them as the centerpiece of an alfresco supper on the patio.

# short ribs braised in balsamic *serves 6–8*

4–5 lb (2–2.5 kg) bone-in beef short ribs, each about 3 inches (7.5 cm) long

Kosher salt and freshly ground pepper

1 tablespoon olive oil

⅔ cup (5 fl oz/160 ml) balsamic vinegar

½ cup (4 fl oz/125 ml) dry red wine

2 tablespoons tomato paste

1 yellow onion, thinly sliced

6 cloves garlic, crushed

10 sprigs fresh flat-leaf parsley, plus ¼ cup (¼ oz/7 g) lightly packed fresh parsley leaves, chopped

2 bay leaves

Trim any excess fat from the short ribs, but leave the silver skin and connective tissue intact.

Arrange the ribs in a single layer in a ceramic or glass baking dish. Sprinkle them with 1–2 tablespoons salt and cover loosely. Refrigerate for at least 3 hours or up to overnight.

Remove the ribs from the refrigerator and pat dry with paper towels. In a large, heavy-bottomed frying pan, heat the olive oil over medium heat. Working in batches to avoid crowding, place the ribs in the pan and sear, turning once, until they develop a golden crust on both sides, about 4 minutes per side. As each batch is done, transfer it to a slow cooker or Dutch oven.

Add the vinegar, wine, tomato paste, onion, garlic, parsley sprigs, and bay leaves to the cooker and stir to combine. Cover and cook on low for 4–6 hours. Uncover the cooker after 4 hours and check one of the thickest ribs; the meat should be very tender and falling off the bone. If not, re-cover and continue cooking, checking again about every 30 minutes.

Using a slotted spoon, transfer the ribs to a platter or large, shallow serving bowl. Discard the parsley sprigs and bay leaves.

Using a large spoon, skim off any fat from the surface of the cooking liquid and discard. Transfer the cooking liquid to a saucepan (reserve the onion in the cooker) and simmer over medium heat until reduced to about ¾ cup (6 fl oz/180 ml), about 10 minutes. Taste and adjust the seasoning.

Spoon the sauce around the ribs. Top with a few spoonfuls of the onion from the cooker, sprinkle with the chopped parsley, and serve right away.

## recipe redux

Since short ribs are best when simmered long and slow, I like to make this dish when I'm feeling like a homebody. I serve it for dinner that night, and then I store the leftovers (they keep in the refrigerator for up to 3 days or in the freezer for up to 1 month). On a busy (or lazy) day, I heat up the leftovers, pull the tender meat off the bones, and stuff it into tortillas with sprigs of cilantro. The combination tastes great with a cold beer.

## — SLOW COOKING —

Slow cooking—food cooked slowly using low heat—is an ideal way to feed a crowd. That's because it typically means you throw stuff in a pot and walk away from it. With very little effort, and often with inexpensive ingredients, preparing a feast for upward of twenty people in a large stove-top pot or in a slow cooker demands no more attention than making dinner for two. And while your meal is gently simmering, you can set a beautiful table, put your energy into making a dessert, or even put your feet up and read a book.

I'm also keen on slow cooking when I want to squirrel away meals for my own little family. Stews, taco meat, and hearty soups often go straight from the Dutch oven into my freezer—or into the freezer of a family recovering from the birth a new baby or of a friend with a broken bone.

You can slow cook with low heat on the stove top or in the oven in a heavy clay or cast-iron pot or Dutch oven. This cookware is often attractive enough to use as a serving dish, as well.

If you have an electric countertop slow cooker, you will enjoy the added benefit of not heating up the kitchen while you cook and the "slow" will be a lot slower. That suits me because one of my favorite meals to make during a heat wave is *carnitas* (braised Mexican pork), which I prepare in my slow cooker. I put a large bone-in pork shoulder into it and add chopped garlic, chipotle chiles, spices, and orange juice. Eight hours and zero effort later, I have enough juicy shredded pork to serve a dozen people.

For general cooking, I recommend having on hand one small pot, a Dutch oven with a 2- to 3-quart (2- to 3-l) capacity, and a larger electric slow cooker or Dutch oven with a capacity of 5 quarts (5 l) or more.

## what can you slow cook?

Curry, gumbo, chili, and other stews; fall-off-the-bone meats like brisket; Moroccan-style chicken; braised short ribs; and shredded meats are all good candidates for slow cooking. But this handy method isn't just for carnivores. Beans, grains, and root vegetables take well to the method, too.

ingredients  Slow cooking is well suited to tougher, inexpensive cuts of meat like stew meat, short ribs, ground meat, chuck roast, and pork shoulder. Sear the meat on all sides before putting it in the slow cooker. (If you are short of time, you can skip this step.) Vegetables tend to cook more slowly than meat, so put them on the bottom and around the sides, adding the tender ones like English peas and squash for the last hour of cooking.

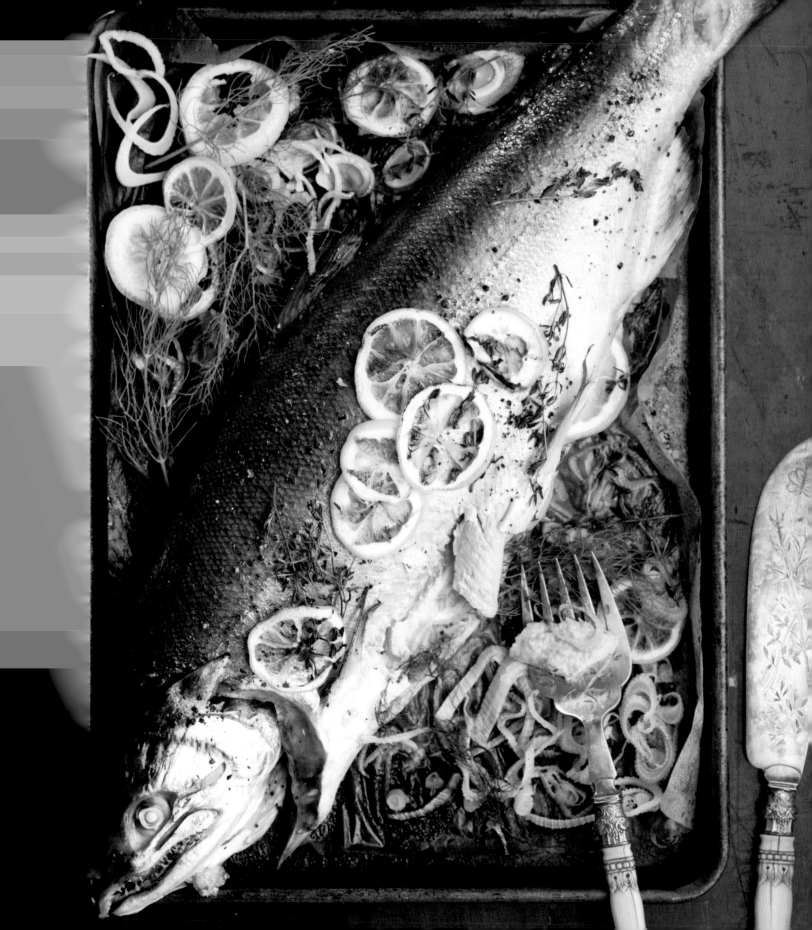

# fennel-roasted whole salmon *serves 10–12*

1 whole salmon, 6–8 lb (3–4 kg),
cleaned by the fishmonger

4 tablespoons (2 fl oz/60 ml) olive oil

Sea salt and freshly ground pepper

2 lemons

1 bunch fresh thyme

3 fennel bulbs, trimmed, cored, and cut
crosswise into slices ½ inch (12 mm) thick,
with handful of fronds reserved

½ cup (4 fl oz/125 ml) dry white wine

Preheat the oven to 500°F (260°C).

Rub the cavity of the salmon with 1 tablespoon of the olive oil. Lightly sprinkle the cavity with salt and pepper.

Using a mandoline or a very sharp knife, cut the lemons crosswise into paper-thin slices. Lay half of the lemon slices inside the cavity of the salmon. Strip a small handful of leaves from the thyme sprigs and scatter them over the lemon slices. Rub the outside of the salmon with another 1 tablespoon olive oil and sprinkle with more salt and pepper.

In a bowl, toss the fennel slices with the remaining 2 tablespoons olive oil to coat thoroughly. Spread the fennel in an even layer on a large, deep, rimmed baking sheet lined with parchment paper or a large roasting pan. Place the fish on top. If just part of the head and/or tail of the fish hangs over the edge(s) of the pan, gently curl the fish to fit inside the pan. If more than that extends over the edge(s) of the pan, you can cut the fish in half crosswise and place the halves side by side. Top the salmon with the remaining lemon slices, arranging them attractively, and place the remaining thyme sprigs and the fennel fronds over and around the fish.

Roast the fish for 15 minutes, then reduce the oven temperature to 425°F (220°C). Pour the wine into the pan all around the fish and continue roasting until the flesh is opaque throughout (use a thin-bladed knife to peek) or an instant-read thermometer inserted into the thickest part registers 130°F (54°C). Start checking at 30 minutes; it may take up to 45 minutes, depending on the size of the fish.

Remove the salmon from the oven and let rest for at least 10 minutes, or let cool to room temperature. Serve the salmon whole, directly from the pan, allowing guests to help themselves to a portion of the fish and some sliced fennel, or transfer the fish to a serving platter and arrange the fennel around the fish. If desired, pass the aioli (right) at the table.

## sustainable choice

It's hard not to like salmon, with its full but mild flavor, meaty texture, beautifully colored flesh, and its high concentration of beneficial omega-3 fatty acids. What is hard to like is that much of it is farmed, and most salmon farming is damaging to the ecosystem. Wild Alaskan salmon is the best choice in terms of sustainability. I try to avoid farmed salmon.

## perfect partner

Accompany the salmon with an easy-to-make creamy, citrusy aioli: In a large bowl, whisk together 2 large egg yolks and a pinch each of sea salt and white pepper until blended. In a slow, steady stream, add ¾ cup (6 fl oz/180 ml) grapeseed oil and ¼ cup (2 fl oz/60 ml) extra-virgin olive oil to the egg yolks, whisking constantly until the mixture is thick and emulsified. Stir in the grated zest of ½ lemon, then thin the aioli with fresh lemon juice until it is the consistency and flavor you like. Serve right away or cover and refrigerate for up to 5 days.

Cioppino and I are both native Californians, although its parents were Italian immigrants who first cooked it up in San Francisco's North Beach in the nineteenth century, and I was raised a century later in the heart of Los Angeles, where hot, lightly spiced fish stews were rare. Nowadays, I like to make this fragrant fisherman's meal myself, and when I am staying by the beach. I use whatever shellfish is fresh off the boat.

# cioppino with toasted baguette *serves 6–8*

1 baguette

5 tablespoons (3 fl oz/80 ml) olive oil

1 large yellow onion, chopped

6 cloves garlic, minced

¼ teaspoon red pepper flakes, or to taste

1 can (28 oz/875 g) diced tomatoes

1 bottle (8 fl oz/250 ml) clam juice

1 cup (8 fl oz/250 ml) dry white wine

¼ cup (¼ oz/7 g) chopped fresh flat-leaf parsley, plus more for garnish

2 tablespoons chopped fresh basil

8 mussels, scrubbed and debearded

16–24 littleneck or cherrystone clams, scrubbed

8 sea scallops

8 shell on large shrimp

1 lb (500 g) crab legs, thawed if frozen, cracked

**fresh take**

Other than two requirements— top-notch seafood and a flavorful broth—almost anything goes when making this hearty stew. I've thrown in leftover corn, chopped fennel, and shallots, and have even used beer in place of the wine. Use this recipe as your guide, but let the bounty of what's available at your local fish and produce markets steer your ultimate ingredient choices.

Preheat the oven to 400°F (200°C).

Cut the baguette on an extreme diagonal into slices about ¾ inch (2 cm) thick. Using about 3 tablespoons of the olive oil, brush one side of each baguette slice liberally. Arrange the slices in a single layer on a baking sheet. Toast in the oven until golden, about 7 minutes. Remove from the oven and wrap in aluminum foil to keep warm.

In a Dutch oven or other large, heavy pot, warm the remaining 2 tablespoons olive oil over medium-high heat. Add the onion and sauté just until translucent, about 1 minute. Add the garlic and red pepper flakes and sauté for 30 seconds. Add the tomatoes and their juices, the clam juice, wine, parsley, and basil. Bring the mixture to a boil. Add all of the shellfish, discarding any mussels or clams that do not close to the touch. Cover, reduce the heat to low, and cook until the mussels and clams have opened and the scallops and shrimp are opaque throughout, about 10 minutes. Discard any mussels or clams that failed to open.

Ladle the stew into individual bowls, dividing the shellfish evenly. Garnish with the parsley, tuck 1 or 2 baguette slices into each bowl, and serve hot with bowls to collect the empty shells.

## — FISH AND SHELLFISH FOR A CROWD —

Whether you're roasting a whole fish, shucking a bag of oysters, grilling or poaching fillets, or making a seafood soup, fish and shellfish are a great choice for serving family style. I match what I decide to make with the setting and the number of guests. Given the woes of overfishing, polluted waters, and damaging fish-farming practices, I always take care when picking which seafood to serve.

**serving a whole fish** One of my favorite ways to prepare fish for a dinner party is to roast one or more whole fish. Branzino (a kind of bass), trout, and salmon are my top picks for this cooking method. If you're not an angler or a chef, you probably don't know how to clean and gut a fish properly, so have the fishmonger do it for you. Leave the head and tail intact. They add flavor and make a nice presentation. I usually budget about ¾–1 pound (375–500 g) of fish per person, depending on the type of fish.

To prepare the fish, stuff the cavity with a mix of aromatics like lemon or orange slices, fennel slices, sliced garlic, or fresh herbs such as thyme, rosemary, dill, or oregano. Most fish roast best in a 400°F (200°C) oven. Line a roasting pan or rimmed baking sheet with parchment paper and place the fish in the pan. A small trout (10 to 12 ounces/275 to 315 g) will take less than 10 minutes, a 1-pound (500-g) branzino will take 10 to 20 minutes, and a large snapper (2 to 3 pounds/1 to 1.5 kg) might take up to 45 minutes. To test for doneness, insert a knife between the backbone and top fillet and lift slightly; the fish is ready if the flesh separates easily from the bone. Alternatively, insert a metal skewer into the center of the fish and then touch the tip of the skewer; it should feel hot.

**serving shellfish** Another easy preparation for a crowd is clams. If you're in an area where clams are native, they're usually inexpensive and, in certain seasons, abundant. Scrub them under cold running water, then throw them on a hot grill, turning them after about 2 minutes with metal tongs. When the shells open, they are done and ready for a platter. I love eating them as is or with lemon wedges and a bottle of Sriracha or other hot sauce.

**don't forget little fish** Anchovies and sardines are two of the best choices in terms of sustainability, plus they are good sources of various nutrients. White anchovies that have been preserved in vinegar *(boquerones)* are one of my favorite nibbles to put out before a meal. Eat them unadorned, or on toasted bread with a drizzle of pesto. Whole fresh sardines are easy to prepare under the broiler. Rub them with olive oil and a pinch of salt, then set a cast-iron griddle or pan under the broiler to preheat for about 10 minutes. Add the sardines and broil until the skin is browned and the tails are charred, about 4 minutes. Serve hot with lemon wedges. If your griddle or pan is large enough, you can cook enough sardines to feed a dozen people in one go.

## a thoughtful choice

By now nearly everyone knows that our oceans are in crisis. These days a trip to the fish counter is an exercise in environmental consciousness, out of concern for both personal health and the health of the oceans. Keep track of the latest data on which fish and shellfish are sustainable choices with a good guide. I like two online sources, the Monterey Bay Aquarium's Seafood Watch and the Blue Ocean Institute's Seafood Guide. They have pocket guides that you can download, print, and carry in your wallet and an app for the iPhone.

Some of the fish that come with the least baggage are anchovies, Pacific halibut, Atlantic mackerel, wild salmon, tilapia, sardines, pollock, cod, and striped bass. Many shellfish make the cut, too, including oysters, mussels, bay scallops, and clams. Freshwater fish like trout are also on the safe list, as long as they come from a clean body of water that has not been overfished.

It may sound extravagant, but poaching fish fillets slowly in olive oil is an excellent way to ensure you don't overcook the fish. Don't worry about oiliness, either. The flesh, which cooks to a toothsome tenderness, is infused with the flavor of the oil but does not absorb the oil itself. During summer, I like to add cherry tomatoes (golden orange Sungold and yellow pear tomatoes are my favorites) to the hot oil to add color and some sweet-tart juices.

# sea bass poached with tomatoes and pesto *serves 4*

for the pesto

1 cup (1 oz/30 g) lightly packed fresh basil, cilantro, or flat-leaf parsley leaves or a combination, plus coarsely chopped herb(s) of choice for garnish

1 teaspoon grated lemon zest

1 tablespoon fresh lemon juice

½ cup (4 fl oz/125 ml) extra-virgin olive oil

4 sea bass fillets, 4–6 oz (125–185 g) each

1 teaspoon sea salt

Extra-virgin olive oil for poaching

1 cup (6 oz/185 g) red or golden orange cherry tomatoes or yellow pear tomatoes, or a combination, halved

**budget saver**

There's no need to waste all of the good olive oil used here for poaching. Let the oil cool, put it in a container, label it "oil for poaching," store it in the refrigerator, and use it a couple more times for poaching fish.

**fresh take**

In the winter, I make the pesto with parsley, and scatter thin kumquat slices and rosemary sprigs in the oil in place of the tomatoes.

To make the pesto, tear or coarsely chop any large herb leaves. In a blender or food processor, combine the herb leaves, lemon juice and zest, and olive oil and process until the herbs are very finely chopped and the pesto is smooth but still has some texture. Stop the machine and scrape down the sides of the container or work bowl as needed. Set aside.

Season the fish on both sides with the salt and arrange the fillets, skin side down, in a frying pan large enough to hold the fish in a single layer without crowding. (You will need a 12-inch/30-cm or larger pan; otherwise, cook the fish in 2 batches or in 2 pans.) Pour enough olive oil into the pan to come halfway up the sides of the fillets. Scatter the tomatoes in the oil.

Place the pan over medium-low heat and cook until the fish begin to turn white around the edges, 2–3 minutes. Spoon some of the poaching oil over the fillets and continue to cook, basting often, until the fish is opaque throughout, 10–15 minutes longer.

Using a slotted spatula, gently lift the fillets from the oil bath and transfer to a platter or individual plates. Scatter the tomato halves over and around the fish. Top each fillet with a few spoonfuls of the pesto and scatter the chopped herb(s) on and around the fish. Serve right away.

This is one of those hits-the-spot dishes. I never knew the merits of a well-made chowder until I lived on the East Coast. I like mine smoky—both the fish and the paprika. Use any smoked fish you like (the dry variety, not smoked salmon or lox), but keep in mind that the best choices for the environment include wild trout, wild mackerel, and certain kinds of cod (often called "whitefish") caught by line, not by trawl net.

# smoked-fish chowder *serves 4–6*

½ cup (3 oz/90 g) chopped pancetta

1 cup (4 oz/125 g) chopped leek

1 cup (4 oz/125 g) finely diced celery

½ cup (2½ oz/75 g) peeled and finely diced carrot

2 teaspoons sea salt

½ teaspoon freshly ground pepper

1 teaspoon smoked paprika

3 cups (24 fl oz/750 ml) dry white wine

½ lb (250 g) red potatoes, unpeeled, diced

1 cup (8 fl oz/250 ml) whole milk

1 cup (8 fl oz/250 ml) heavy cream

1 lb (500 g) dry-smoked fish fillets such as haddock, whitefish, trout, pollock, or mackerel, skin removed

½ lemon (optional)

2 hard-boiled eggs, peeled and chopped

½ cup (½ oz/75 g) finely diced red onion

Small dill sprigs for garnish

**perfect partners**

Hearty and full of protein, this chowder doesn't need much more to make it a meal. A loaf of crusty bread goes without saying, but I also like to serve it with either a green salad or just a plate of vegetables fresh from the garden, like carrots, radishes, or sugar snap peas. Accompany with ale or a crisp white wine.

In a heavy saucepan, cook the pancetta over medium-low heat until it starts to crisp, 5–7 minutes. Remove from the heat. Using a slotted spoon, transfer the pancetta to paper towels to drain.

Add the leek, celery, carrot, salt, pepper, and paprika to the rendered fat in the pan. Return to medium-low heat and cook, stirring constantly, until tender, about 5 minutes. Add the wine, raise the heat to high, and bring to a simmer. Reduce the heat to low, add the potatoes, and cook just until tender, about 10 minutes. Remove the pot from the heat and stir in the milk, cream, fish, and reserved pancetta.

Let the chowder stand at room temperature for 1 hour to allow the flavors to develop. When ready to serve, reheat gently over low heat. Taste and adjust the seasoning, adding a few drops of lemon juice if it needs a touch of brightness.

Ladle the chowder into warmed individual bowls and garnish with the hard-boiled eggs, red onion, and dill. Serve right away.

If anything begs for slow cooking, it's chili. By simmering it at a snail's pace, the sauce develops a complex flavor and the meat blends into the sauce. Texans point out that "real" chili has no tomatoes and no beans, but I include both of them because they make my chili a one-bowl meal.

# black bean and beef chili *serves 8–10*

1 tablespoon olive oil

1½ large yellow onions, chopped

3 lb (1.5 kg) ground beef

1 lb (500 g) dried black beans, soaked overnight

1 can (28 oz/875 g) plum tomatoes

¼ cup (2 fl oz/60 ml) cider vinegar or red wine vinegar

¼ cup (⅓ oz/10 g) chopped fresh oregano

6 large cloves garlic, chopped

2 tablespoons ground cinnamon

1 tablespoon mild chili powder

1 tablespoon ground cumin

1 teaspoon cayenne pepper, or to taste

4 cups (32 fl oz/1 l) beef stock or low-sodium broth, heated

1 cup (8 oz/250 g) sour cream

1 red onion, minced

½ cup (½ oz/15 g) lightly packed fresh cilantro leaves

2 limes, each cut into 8 wedges

## make ahead

One thing that most people agree on is that chili gets better if it has a chance to rest before you eat it. So, if possible, make the chili a day ahead and reheat it just before serving. Sometimes I divide a batch of chili into amounts that will feed my family of three for dinner and freeze the containers for up to 1 month. Then, at the end of a busy day, dinner is ready in minutes.

In a Dutch oven or other large, heavy-bottomed pot, heat the olive oil over medium-high heat. Add the yellow onions and sauté until golden, about 5 minutes. Add the beef and cook, stirring and breaking up the clumps with a wooden spoon, until no longer pink, about 3 minutes.

Drain the black beans, rinse well, and drain again. Add the beans, tomatoes, vinegar, oregano, garlic, cinnamon, chili powder, cumin, and cayenne to the pot and stir to combine. Add the stock, raise the heat to high, and bring to a boil, stirring occasionally. Reduce the heat to maintain a very low simmer and cook, uncovered, stirring occasionally and skimming off the fat that rises to the surface, until the beans are tender and the meat has broken up into the sauce, about 2 hours. Taste and adjust the seasoning.

Ladle the chili into warmed individual bowls and let diners garnish portions with the sour cream, red onion, cilantro, and lime wedges. Serve hot.

I used to buy dough from my neighborhood pizzeria. When it changed hands, the new owner would no longer sell me the dough rounds. Good thing, it turns out, because I might not have gotten into making pizza dough. I'm glad I was pushed, as it's much easier—and the dough more forgiving—than I ever imagined.

# basic pizza *makes 2 large pizzas*

1 package (2½ teaspoons) active dry yeast

¾ cup (6 fl oz/180 ml) warm water (about 110°F/43°F), plus more as needed

1 teaspoon sugar

1 tablespoon plus 1 teaspoon extra-virgin olive oil

3 cups (15 oz/470 g) bread flour or all-purpose flour, or a mixture, plus more for kneading

1 teaspoon salt

1–2 tablespoons semolina flour

In a small bowl, sprinkle the yeast over the warm water and let stand until foamy, about 5 minutes. Stir in the sugar and 1 tablespoon of the olive oil.

In a large bowl, whisk together the flour and salt. Make a well in the center, pour in the yeast mixture, and mix with a wooden spoon just until the dough barely holds together. Add more warm water, 1 teaspoon at a time, if needed to get the right consistency.

Turn the dough out onto a lightly floured work surface. With flour-dusted hands, knead until smooth and elastic, about 10 minutes, then shape into a ball. Grease a large bowl with the remaining 1 teaspoon oil, add the dough, turn to coat with the oil, and cover the bowl with plastic wrap. Let the dough rise in a warm spot until doubled in size, 1–2 hours.

Divide the dough in half, knead each half into a ball, cover with a kitchen towel, and let rest for about 20 minutes. Meanwhile, place a pizza stone or a large baking sheet turned upside down in the oven and preheat to 500°F (260°C) or as high as it will go.

On a lightly floured work surface, flatten 1 dough ball and roll out into a circle, oval, or rectangle ¼–½ inch (6–12 mm) thick. Transfer to a pizza peel or sheet of parchment paper dusted with semolina. Top with toppings of choice (see page 133), then quickly slide the pizza onto the stone or baking sheet. If using parchment, lay the parchment on the stone or pan, bake for a few minutes, then pull the paper free.

Bake until the top is bubbling and the edges are deep brown in spots, 5–9 minutes. Remove from the oven. If using uncooked toppings, such as greens, herbs, or cured meats, add them, then serve at once. Repeat with the remaining dough.

## make ahead
To make the dough ahead of time, let it rise slowly in the refrigerator for at least 8 hours or up to overnight.

## make more to store
Once you master the technique, you'll want to double or triple this recipe and stash the extra dough in the freezer for an easy fix the next time a pizza craving hits. You can wrap either balls of the dough or rolled-out rounds in plastic wrap and freeze them for up to 1 month. Let the dough come to room temperature before rolling out the balls or topping the rounds.

## — PIZZA FOR A CROWD —

I confess: I'm enthralled with pizza. No matter the time of year or the occasion, I love to make it. I serve pizza for weekend lunches, as a first course at dinner parties, and even for breakfast with an egg on top. I'll try any topping once. I like pizza's versatility and how it gets people involved in cooking in a really gritty way.

I also like to make it a group activity. Some folks can roll the dough—the brave ones can try tossing it—and others can arrange the toppings. Friends can pair up and make half-and-half pizzas, with two different toppings. Kids can pull off small balls of dough and make their own little pizzas. Here are a few tips that will help guarantee delicious pies.

**start with good dough** The dough is important. Make it yourself (page 131), or ask a local pizzeria if you can buy a lump or two. If you are making your own dough, bread flour generally works better than all-purpose flour because it is high in gluten, which contributes to elasticity and loft. But either is fine, so don't fuss over the flour. When the mood to make pizza dough hits me, I try to do large batches so I have some to freeze for another day.

**topping tips** Don't overload the pizza with toppings. I know because I've done it. Too many toppings lead to a heavy, wet pizza and a soggy crust. I usually limit myself to three or four. The order of things is generally dough, sauce, cheese, then meat and vegetables and any extra cheese. When the pizza is done, you can add fresh toppings like chopped herbs and greens.

**high heat** I've made pizzas in centuries-old outdoor ovens in Tuscany and in cheap toaster ovens in cramped New York City apartments and they are all good. Use what you have and strive for the highest heat possible, because high heat is what gives you that special pizzeria-style crisp crust.

Most of us aren't lucky enough to have a wood-burning brick oven at home, but you can mimic that environment with a hot oven (turn it up as high as it goes, 500° or 550°F (260° or 290°C) on most ovens) and a baking stone. The stone pulls moisture out of the dough, making that crisp bottom. If you don't have a stone, use a preheated baking sheet.

You can also cook pizza on a grill. You need a clean grill rack that has been oiled, and a dough round of uniform thickness. Use the grill cover to control the heat. Grill one side of the crust, then flip, quickly add the toppings, and continue grilling until the bottom is a deep golden brown and the toppings are bubbling.

## toppings

Here is a list of some of my favorite pizza toppings. I know that most people have strong opinions about what should go on a pizza, so these are suggestions only. In other words, I am not about to stand between a pizza lover and his or her traditional toppings.

**sauces**  tomato sauce, pesto, béchamel

**cheeses**  mozzarella, creamy Gorgonzola, fresh ricotta, Parmesan, fontina, fresh goat cheese

**protein**  sausage, pancetta, bresaola, anchovies, sardines, toasted chopped walnuts

**vegetables and fruits**  tomatoes of all shapes, types, and sizes; braised fennel; sautéed onions; sliced figs; halved grapes; potato slices; zucchini slices; eggplant slices; roasted garlic

**fresh finishes (added to cooked pizza)**  salt and freshly ground pepper, chopped arugula, chopped spinach, chopped fresh herbs (basil, rosemary, tarragon, oregano, thyme), prosciutto

Okay, so there are only four true herbs here—but I count the celery leaves as a fifth because they are so delicate and full of green herbal nuances. This pesto has a looser look and feel, and likewise dances differently on the palate, than traditional pulverized pestos. The herbs are chopped, which keeps the flavors bright and allows them to stay distinct even as they mingle.

# spaghetti with five-herb pesto *serves 4–6*

Sea salt and freshly ground pepper

1 cup (1 oz/30 g) lightly packed fresh basil leaves

1 cup (1 oz/30 g) lightly packed fresh flat-leaf parsley leaves

2 tablespoons lightly packed fresh tarragon leaves

2 tablespoons lightly packed fresh sage leaves

½ teaspoon fresh lemon juice

1 clove garlic, coarsely chopped

½ cup (2 oz/60 g) freshly grated Parmesan cheese

½ cup (2½ oz/75 g) pine nuts, lightly toasted

½ cup (4 fl oz/125 ml) extra-virgin olive oil

1 lb (500 g) spaghetti

½ cup (½ oz/15 g) lightly packed celery leaves

**add flavor**

Although pasta with pesto is one of my favorite meatless dinner options, once in a while I crave a bit of protein, which I satisfy by topping the dish with crisp pancetta cubes or chewy ribbons of prosciutto.

**pack to go**

For a picnic or summer potluck, I turn this hot dish into a pasta salad. I cook penne, drain and cool it under running cold water, and then toss it with the pesto. I sometimes add some cooked fresh vegetables; green beans and asparagus, cut into 1-inch (2.5-cm) lengths, are two of my favorites. Or, I add torn pieces of fresh mozzarella and roasted chicken.

Bring a large pot three-fourths full of lightly salted water to a boil over medium-high heat.

Finely chop the basil, parsley, tarragon, and sage and place in a bowl. Sprinkle in the lemon juice and stir to coat the herbs with the juice.

Combine the garlic, Parmesan, and pine nuts in a blender or food processor. With the machine running, add the olive oil in a slow, steady stream and process until the mixture is creamy and blended. Pour the oil mixture into the bowl with the herbs and stir to combine.

Add the spaghetti to the boiling water and cook, stirring occasionally to prevent sticking, until the pasta is al dente, 10–12 minutes or according to package directions. Drain the pasta and transfer to a serving bowl. Toss with the pesto, a pinch or two of salt, and a few grinds of pepper. Top with the celery leaves and serve right away.

The frittata, an Italian cousin to the French quiche (minus the crust, of course), is perfect picnic fare: sturdy enough to travel and easy to transport. Other vegetables and cheeses can be used here, such as arugula and fontina or Swiss chard and provolone. This is a good make-ahead dish, too: it will keep in the refrigerator for up to 2 days.

# herbed spinach and emmentaler frittata *serves 4–6*

8 large eggs

1½ cups (6 oz/185 g) shredded Emmentaler cheese

Sea salt and freshly ground pepper

2 tablespoons unsalted butter

1 shallot, chopped

1 tablespoon chopped fresh basil

1 tablespoon chopped fresh thyme

1 tablespoon fresh chopped flat-leaf parsley

10 oz (315 g) baby spinach

**make it a meal**

In the summer when it can be too hot to cook, I often make a simple frittata and serve it with a chopped green salad, sliced tomatoes, a crusty baguette, and a bottle of chilled rosé. For dessert, I'll set out platters of whatever fresh fruit looked best at the market that day.

Position a rack 5–6 inches (13–15 cm) from the heat source and preheat the broiler. In a bowl, lightly whisk together the eggs and 1 cup (4 oz/125 g) of the cheese. Season lightly with salt and pepper and set aside.

In a well-seasoned 10- or 12-inch (25- or 30-cm) cast-iron frying pan, melt the butter over medium-high heat. Add the shallot and sauté until fragrant, about 2 minutes. Add the basil, thyme, and parsley and sauté for 30 seconds longer. Add the spinach and cook, stirring, until the spinach leaves are completely wilted, about 2 minutes.

Pour the egg mixture into the pan. Reduce the heat to medium and cook, without disturbing the egg mixture and adjusting the heat as needed to prevent the bottom from burning, until the frittata is set around the edges, 5–10 minutes. Sprinkle the remaining ½ cup (2 oz/60 g) cheese evenly over the top.

Transfer the pan to the broiler and cook until the frittata is nearly set in the center and deep golden brown on top, about 4 minutes, watching carefully to prevent burning.

Let the frittata stand for at least 10 minutes or until cooled to room temperature. Cut into wedges to serve.

This frittata assumes a Spanish identity with the addition of chorizo sausage, Manchego cheese, and *piquillo* peppers. The latter are small, slender, mildly spicy red peppers traditionally grown in northern Spain, where they are roasted, peeled, and packed into jars. Look for them in Spanish markets or specialty-food stores.

# chorizo and piquillo pepper frittata *serves 4–6*

8 large eggs

Sea salt and freshly ground pepper

2 tablespoons olive oil

2 Yukon gold potatoes, peeled and diced (about 2 cups/10 oz/315 g)

6 oz (185 g) chorizo, casing removed

1 yellow onion, diced

1 large ripe tomato, cored, seeded, and diced

¾ cup (3¾ oz/110 g) seeded and coarsely chopped jarred *piquillo* peppers

¾ cup (3 oz/90 g) shredded Manchego cheese

**dress it up**
Cut this frittata into 1-inch (2.5-cm) squares and you'll have a wine-friendly appetizer. To stay with the Spanish theme, serve the frittata bites with a dry sherry or a crisp white Albariño and set out bowls of olives and Marcona almonds.

Position a rack 5–6 inches (13–15 cm) from the heat source and preheat the broiler. In a bowl, lightly whisk together the eggs, season lightly with salt and pepper and set aside.

In a well-seasoned 10- or 12-inch (25- or 30-cm) cast-iron frying pan, heat the olive oil over medium-high heat. Add the potatoes and cook, stirring occasionally, until golden and crisp on the edges, about 8 minutes. Using a slotted spoon, transfer the potatoes to a plate.

Add the chorizo to the pan and cook, breaking up the sausage into a uniform crumble with the side of a spoon, until lightly browned, 5–7 minutes. Add the onion and cook, stirring often, until translucent, 3–4 minutes longer. Pour off and discard the fat in the pan.

Add the tomato and peppers to the pan and stir to combine. Return the potatoes to the pan and toss gently to mix. Pour the eggs into the pan. Reduce the heat to medium and cook, without disturbing and adjusting the heat as needed to prevent the bottom from burning, until the frittata is set around the edges, about 5–10 minutes. Sprinkle the cheese evenly over the top.

Transfer the pan to the broiler and cook until the frittata is nearly set in the center and deep golden brown on top, about 4 minutes, watching carefully to prevent burning.

Let the frittata stand for at least 10 minutes or until cooled to room temperature. Cut into wedges to serve.

Earthy mushrooms and bits of salty ham stud this silky baked pasta dish with bursts of flavor. If you cannot find thin, straight-edged no-boil lasagna sheets at your market, try a shop that specializes in Italian foods. You don't want ruffled edges on this rustic dish.

# white lasagna with mushrooms and prosciutto *serves 6–8*

½ cup (4 oz/125 g) unsalted butter, plus more for greasing

½ cup (2½ oz/75 g) unbleached all-purpose flour

½ teaspoon freshly grated nutmeg

4 cups (32 fl oz/1 l) whole milk

1 cup (8 fl oz/250 ml) chicken stock or low-sodium broth

½ cup (4 fl oz/125 ml) Marsala

2 large eggs, lightly beaten

1¾ cups (7 oz/220 g) shredded fontina cheese

Sea salt and freshly ground white pepper

4 tablespoons (2 fl oz/60 ml) olive oil, plus more if needed

1 small leek, white and tender green parts only, thinly sliced

¾ lb (375 g) white mushrooms, brushed clean and sliced

½ lb (250 g) thinly sliced prosciutto, chopped

2 tablespoons chopped fresh basil

12 sheets no-boil lasagna, each about 7 by 3½ inches (18 by 9 cm)

½ cup (2 oz/60 g) freshly grated Parmesan cheese

**save time**

You can use dried lasagna noodles in this recipe (follow the instructions on the box to precook), but no-boil noodles are this harried cook's solution to lasagna for dinner. They cut down on the time and the space you need to prepare the dish (no need to lay the precooked noodles on a flat surface before layering), and you won't be able to tell the difference in taste or texture.

**make ahead**

You can assemble the lasagna, cover it tightly, and store it in the refrigerator for up to 1 day, or double-wrap it and put it in the freezer for up to 1 month.

Preheat the oven to 350°F (180°C). Butter an 8-by-11-inch (20-by-28-cm) baking dish.

In a large saucepan, melt the butter over medium-low heat. Stir in the flour and cook, whisking constantly, for about 3 minutes. Whisk in the nutmeg. Raise the heat to medium-high and gradually whisk in the milk and stock. Bring the mixture to a boil and continue whisking until thickened and smooth, 10–15 minutes. Remove from the heat and let cool, stirring occasionally, until warm. Stir in the Marsala, eggs, and 1 cup (4 oz/125 g) of the fontina until the cheese melts and the sauce is smooth. Season with salt and white pepper. Set aside.

In a large frying pan, heat 2 tablespoons of the olive oil over medium-high heat. Add the leek and sauté just until wilted, about 3 minutes. Transfer to a bowl. Add the remaining 2 tablespoons olive oil to the pan. When the oil is hot, add the mushrooms and sauté, stirring, until golden, about 5 minutes. Add the prosciutto and basil and cook, stirring, for 1 minute longer.

Spread about 1½ cups (12 fl oz/375 ml) of the cheese sauce evenly over the bottom of the prepared baking dish. Spoon about one-third of the mushroom mixture evenly over the sauce, then arrange 4 of the lasagna sheets over the top. Repeat these layers twice. Spread the remaining sauce over the top layer, then sprinkle the remaining ¾ cup (3 oz/95 g) fontina and the Parmesan evenly over the top. Bake until the top is golden and the juices are bubbling, about 45 minutes. Let the lasagna cool for 15 to 30 minutes, cut into squares, and serve right away.

# Vegetables and Sides

Spring vegetable ragout • Braised artichokes with lemon, mint, and olives • **Cooking seasonally** • Maple-glazed sweet potato wedges • Squash ribbon puff pastry tart • Israeli couscous with porcini and arugula • **Grains for a crowd** • Balsamic-glazed roasted radicchio with walnuts • Grilled asparagus with bacon vinaigrette • Roasted stuffed tomatoes • **Summer tomatoes** • Toasted sesame sugar snap peas • Haricots verts with almond pesto Caramelized cauliflower steaks • Roasted broccoli with red pepper flakes and garlic • Cheesy acini de pepe with fresh herbs • Endive gratin • Rosemary white beans with fontina • Smashed potatoes • Skillet cornbread

Dinner doesn't get more seasonal than this springtime dish—a celebration of green with clean, bright flavors. I like to alter the ingredients depending on what I find at the farmers' market, adding or substituting green garlic, ramps, sugar snap peas, and/or chervil for the ingredients listed below. If I am lucky enough to score fresh morels, they go in with the leeks.

# spring vegetable ragout *serves 4–6*

1 lb (500 g) fava beans, shelled

1 lb (500 g) asparagus, woody ends snapped off

4 tablespoons (2 oz/60 g) unsalted butter

1 small leek, white and tender green parts only, sliced

3 cloves garlic, chopped

1 cup (8 fl oz/250 ml) chicken stock or low-sodium broth

1 cup (8 fl oz/250 ml) dry white wine

1 lb (500 g) English peas, shelled

1 cup (2 oz/60 g) torn pea shoots

1 tablespoon chopped fresh mint

1 tablespoon chopped fresh basil

1 tablespoon chopped fresh chives

Sea salt and freshly ground pepper

### recipe redux

This dish usually disappears quickly, but if you are lucky enough to have leftovers, toss them into hot pasta with strips of prosciutto and grated pecorino; stir them into risotto; mix them with cooked farro, Israeli couscous, or quinoa; or use them as a topping for crostini, dressed with a drizzle of balsamic vinegar.

### fresh take

For an even brighter-flavored dish, stir 1½ teaspoons grated lemon or orange zest into the vegetables just before seasoning with salt and pepper.

Bring a saucepan three-fourths full of water to a boil over high heat. Have ready a large bowl of ice water. Add the fava beans to the boiling water and cook for 2 minutes. Quickly drain in a colander, then immediately plunge the beans into the ice water. Drain, and when cool enough to handle, slip the outer skin from each bean. Set aside. Cut the asparagus into 1½-inch (4-cm) lengths. Set aside.

In a large sauté pan, melt the butter over medium-high heat. Add the leek and sauté until soft, about 1 minute. Add the garlic and sauté for 30 seconds longer. Stir in the stock and wine and bring to a boil. Add the peas and asparagus and return to a boil. Reduce the heat to medium-low and simmer for 5 minutes. Using a slotted spoon, transfer the peas and asparagus to a warmed serving bowl. Raise the heat to medium-high and simmer the liquid in the pan until reduced by about three-fourths, about 5 minutes.

Add the fava beans, pea shoots, mint, basil, and chives to the bowl with the peas and asparagus and toss to mix thoroughly. Pour the hot liquid in the pan over the vegetables and toss again. Season with salt and pepper. Serve right away.

Artichokes always bring visual—even architectural—interest to the table. Here, the addition of olives and mint to a simple braise promises to excite even the most die-hard artichoke fans. This earthy vegetable is typically thought of as a springtime treat, but it has a short fall season, too. I like to make this dish to serve alongside braised or roasted chicken when the weather turns cool. When you braise, rather than steam, the artichokes, they are continuously bathed in the flavorful cooking juices, turning them soft and velvety.

# braised artichokes with lemon, mint, and olives *serves 6–8*

4 artichokes

¼ cup (2 fl oz/60 ml) fresh lemon juice

5 cloves garlic, thinly sliced

½ cup (4 fl oz/125 ml) olive oil

½ cup (4 fl oz/125 ml) chicken stock or low-sodium broth

2 large shallots, minced

Sea salt and freshly ground pepper

½ cup (2½ oz/75 g) pitted Kalamata olives

½ cup (½ oz/15 g) coarsely torn fresh mint

1 lemon, cut into wedges

### ingredient note

If using more-mature artichokes, the outer leaves may be tender only at the base, but the inner leaves should be soft enough to consume whole or nearly whole. Substitute baby artichokes when you can find them, cutting them into halves instead of into quarters. If they are young enough, there won't even be a fuzzy choke to cut out.

Preheat the oven to 375°F (190°C).

Using a large serrated knife, trim off about 1 inch (2.5 cm) of the tops and the stem ends of each artichoke. Using scissors, trim off the thorny tips of each outer leaf. Using the serrated knife, quarter the artichokes lengthwise, then scoop out the fuzzy chokes with the tip of a small spoon. Place the artichoke quarters in a baking dish or Dutch oven, sprinkle with lemon juice, and toss to coat. Scatter the garlic slices on top.

In a bowl, whisk together the olive oil, chicken stock, and shallots. Season to taste with salt and pepper. Pour the mixture evenly over the artichokes. Cover the dish with aluminum foil and place in the oven. Bake until the artichokes are tender when pierced with a fork, about 50 minutes. Uncover, add the olives and mint, and toss to combine. Return to the oven and bake, uncovered, for 5 minutes longer to heat the olives through and to blend the flavors.

Transfer the artichokes to a serving dish and pour the pan juices over the top. Serve right away and pass the lemon wedges at the table.

## — COOKING SEASONALLY —

While I'm happy that terms like *locavore* and *farm to table* have become popular over the last decade or so, it saddens me that we even need a term for this sensible approach to eating. Has the world grown so big and complicated that we must fight against the riptide of large-scale factory farming and all that comes with it in order to ensure we are eating foods whose safety and nutrition have not been compromised by the way they were grown? Unfortunately, the answer is yes.

**a simple way to cook**  The good news is that it is not hard to eat locally and seasonally. Cooking in season doesn't require any extra skill. What it does require is a commitment to cook with what the earth naturally produces at any given time of year. It means letting the ingredients available to you from your local farmer or farmers' market dictate how you eat.

Becoming a member of a CSA (Community Supported Agriculture), a farm that sells shares of its crops at the beginning of each season and regularly delivers or offers for pick up a box of fresh, seasonal crops straight from the land, is another easy way to guarantee you are eating in season and locally. There are CSAs for fruits and vegetables, for dairy, and even for meats. With planning, you can eat this way year-round.

One thing we can all do is try to buy directly from the source as much as possible. In other words, if you are buying from farmers and food producers near your home, chances are you are eating seasonally and locally. It is encouraging to see that some vendors in farmers' markets in major U.S. cities are now accepting food stamps. It's important that farmers' markets no longer be seen as elite institutions. Stocking the pantry with farm-fresh products is how the world used to eat, no matter the shoppers' economic status. The more support farmers get, the more land will be preserved, and the more access everyone will have to fresh, seasonal, local ingredients.

## no farmers' market nearby?

Use a reliable seasonal eating chart. I like the Natural Resources Defense Council's Simple Steps chart, which lists in-season produce by state and month and includes a farmers' market finder.

One thing is clear: food sourced locally and seasonally tastes better. A tomato, for example, when grown in the environment it craves—long, hot days—and picked shortly before it is consumed tastes entirely different from one grown in winter with artificial light and heat and picked green and hard so it will survive its long journey to a consumer who can't wait until summer for tomatoes.

So what's to eat in winter? For folks in colder northern climates, the winter can be a daunting time to eat seasonally. The best advice I have is to make friends with apples, pears, carrots, beets, turnips, cabbage, and potatoes, which isn't such a bad crowd. Plus, grains, good-quality meats, nuts, and cheeses can boost the appeal of a meal of dead-of-winter root vegetables. Finally, don't worry—spring is around the corner.

These burnt-orange sweet potatoes make a great dish when you're feeding a crowd—festive enough for a holiday or fast enough for a snowy-day supper. The recipe is easily multiplied and is so simple, you can ask almost anyone to prepare it if you have other dishes to tend to. Consider this the basic formula, but you can also dress up the sweet spuds with spices like ground fennel, ground ginger, or red pepper flakes.

# maple-glazed sweet potato wedges *serves 4–6*

3 sweet potatoes, about
1½ lb (750 g) total weight

2 tablespoons pure maple syrup

1 tablespoon olive oil

1 teaspoon kosher salt

½ teaspoon freshly ground pepper

½ teaspoon chopped fresh rosemary

Preheat the oven to 450°F (230°C).

Cut the sweet potatoes lengthwise into uniform wedges about 1 inch (2.5 cm) wide. In a large bowl, whisk together the maple syrup, olive oil, salt, pepper, and rosemary. Add the potato wedges and toss to coat evenly.

Arrange the wedges in a single layer in a roasting pan or on a baking sheet and drizzle with any maple syrup mixture left in the bowl.

Roast for 20 minutes. Carefully remove the pan from the oven. Turn the wedges with a spatula or by shaking the pan, then continue roasting until fork-tender, about 15 minutes longer. Transfer to a platter and let cool slightly. Taste and adjust the seasoning. Serve warm.

**dress it up**

Sometimes I'm just in the mood for creamy, silky, mashed sweet potatoes. I consider a mash fit for company if it is laced with interesting flavors. To transform this dish, peel the sweet potatoes, cut into 1-inch (2.5-cm) cubes, and cook in boiling salted water for 5–7 minutes. Drain, add 2 tablespoons room-temperature unsalted butter, and mash until smooth. Swirl in the maple syrup mixture and serve right away.

This showcase for the bounty of the summer garden is easy to make because you use purchased puff pastry. If you have time, arrange the squash slices into an eye-catching pattern. For example, if you cut the squashes lengthwise, as I have done here, you can weave them into a lattice. Or, you can thinly cut the squash crosswise and make an overlapping scalloped pattern with the various-size rounds. In both cases, a mandoline is the ideal tool to achieve thin, uniform slices.

# squash ribbon puff pastry tart *serves 6–8*

½ cup (2 oz/60 g) freshly grated Parmesan cheese

¼ cup (2 oz/60 g) mascarpone cheese

1 large egg

2 tablespoons heavy cream

1 teaspoon finely chopped fresh mint

1 teaspoon finely chopped fresh thyme

Sea salt and freshly ground pepper

All-purpose flour for dusting

1 sheet puff pastry, about ½ lb (250 g), thawed according to package directions if frozen

1 large zucchini and 1 large yellow crookneck squash, trimmed and very thinly sliced lengthwise with a mandoline or vegetable peeler

1 teaspoon olive oil

Preheat the oven to 375°F (190°C). Line a baking sheet with parchment paper.

In a bowl, combine ¼ cup (1 oz/30 g) of the Parmesan, the mascarpone, egg, cream, mint, thyme, and a little salt and pepper and stir until well mixed. Set aside.

On a lightly floured work surface, roll out the puff pastry into a 9-by-13-inch (23-by-33-cm) rectangle about ⅛ inch (3 mm) thick. Transfer the pastry to the prepared baking sheet. Using the tip of a sharp knife, score a border about ¾ inch (2 cm) in from the edge all the way around the pastry sheet, piercing only the top few layers. Spread the cheese mixture evenly over the pastry inside the border, then arrange the squash slices diagonally across the tart. Brush the squash slices and the pastry edges with the olive oil.

Bake the tart for 15 minutes, then sprinkle with the remaining ¼ cup (1 oz/30 g) Parmesan. Continue to bake until the cheese is melted and the pastry is golden, about 15 minutes longer. Let cool on the pan on a wire rack for 5 minutes. Cut into pieces and serve warm.

*See page 153 for photo*

## fresh take

I also like to top this tart with eggplant and feta in place of the zucchini and mascarpone. I salt the eggplant slices, let them stand in a colander for 15 minutes or so, then blot off the released water before using. Because the feta is chunkier, I give it a whirl in a mini food processor with the Parmesan, egg, and cream, then stir in the herbs and seasonings before spreading the mixture on the puff pastry.

## dress it up

I usually serve this tart rustic style—like I do pizza—on a well-worn wooden board. But if you want a fancier look, cut out rounds from the baked tart with a fluted-edged pastry cutter and serve them on a cake stand or other attractive serving tray.

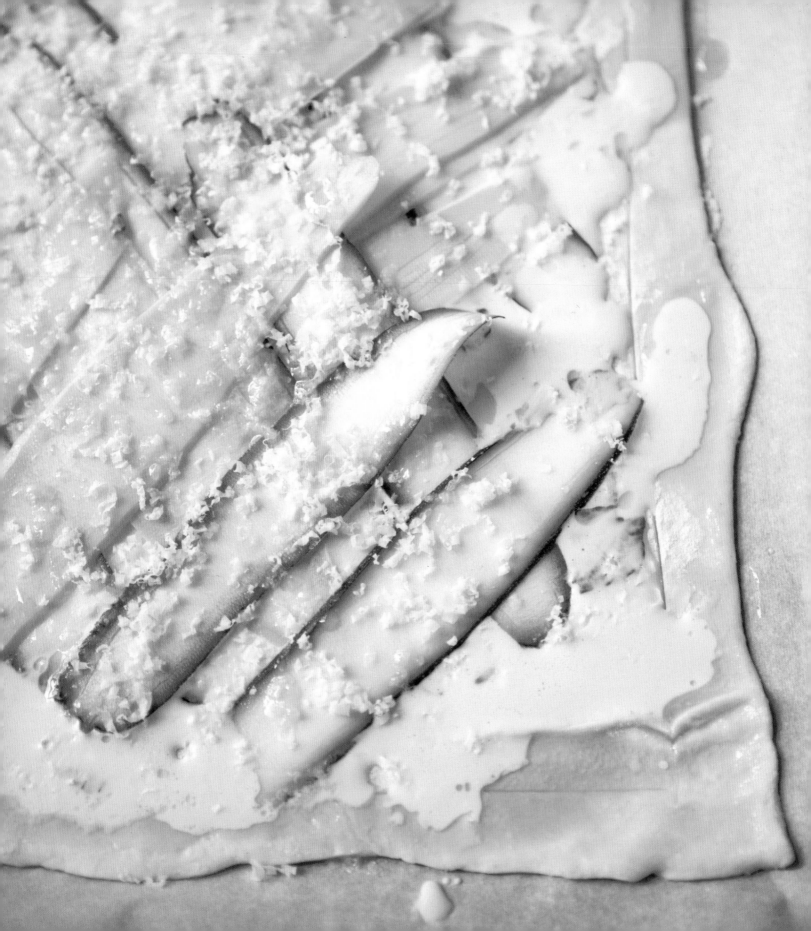

The deep, dark flavors of smoked mozzarella and porcini mushrooms are meant for each other. Toss the two with a quick-cooking grain like couscous and some lacy greens like arugula and you have a dish that's short on prep time and long on flavor, texture, and visual appeal. The corn makes this a summer dish. But if you crave it in winter, you can use 1 cup (6 oz/185 g) thawed frozen corn.

# israeli couscous with porcini and arugula *serves 4–6*

½ cup (½ oz/15 g) dried porcini mushrooms

3 tablespoons olive oil

1 cup (8 oz/250 g) Israeli couscous

2 cups (16 fl oz/500 ml) chicken stock or low-sodium broth, warmed

2 ears corn, husks and silks removed

2 handfuls baby arugula, tough stems removed

¼ lb (125 g) smoked mozzarella cheese, cut into ¼-inch (6-mm) dice

1 tablespoon champagne vinegar

Sea salt and freshly ground pepper

**double for a crowd**

This recipe doubles or triples easily for a big brunch or barbecue. When bringing to a party, I like to keep the arugula in a separate container and stir it in just before serving so that the tender leaves don't wilt.

**fresh take**

If I want my carbs to be more nutritious, I use farro, barley, or quinoa, or a mixture, in place of the couscous. The earthiness of the farro pairs especially well with the rich, meaty porcini.

Put the porcini in a small heatproof bowl. In a small saucepan, bring ½ cup (4 fl oz/125 ml) water to a boil over high heat. Pour the boiling water over the mushrooms. Set aside and let steep until the mushrooms are soft and plump, about 20 minutes.

Meanwhile, in a large saucepan, heat 1 tablespoon of the olive oil over medium-high heat. Add the couscous and toast, stirring constantly, until lightly golden, about 5 minutes. Pour in the stock. If necessary, add hot water to cover by ½ inch (3 mm). Bring to a boil, reduce the heat to medium, and cook until al dente, about 10 minutes. Drain thoroughly in a fine-mesh sieve and transfer to a large salad bowl.

Cut the kernels off the ears of corn and add to the bowl with the couscous. Drain the mushrooms and chop into bite-size pieces. Add to the bowl. Add the arugula, mozzarella, and corn.

In a small bowl, whisk together the remaining 2 tablespoons olive oil and the vinegar. Pour over the salad and toss until the ingredients are well distributed and coated with the dressing. Season generously with salt and pepper, toss again gently, and serve right away.

## — GRAINS FOR A CROWD —

The reasons to eat grains are many. First and most important, they are packed with nutrients. Grains are also the ultimate meal stretcher. When all I have is a small handful of salad greens for four, but suddenly the head count is eight, that salad easily transforms into a leafy grain salad to feed us all, with leftovers. Grains will do the same favors for soups: they can double the yield, plus add an earthy flavor and texture boost. And there are dozens of grains to choose from.

Some grains like couscous and quinoa cook up in a snap. Others like wheat berries, pearl barley, and certain types of rice take more planning. The good news is that most dried grains yield double to triple their volume when cooked and will hold in the refrigerator for a few days. They are also incredibly easy to prepare and simmer unattended while you finesse the rest of the meal.

Grains are cheap, so stock up (store grains in sealed glass jars) and start experimenting to find those whose flavor and texture you like. Try out different types to see which add the most to your meals. Giving a recipe for grains seems almost unnecessary, since all you need to know is how to cook them. You can't go wrong by adding a grain to just about any soup or salad, or dressing it up with a little fruity olive oil, salt, and pepper and serving it as a side dish to meats, poultry, or fish.

When I want to give a grain a starring role, I make a salad. See Israeli couscous salad (page 155) for ideas on how to incorporate vegetables. Raw or roasted vegetables, shredded cooked meats, toasted nuts, chopped herbs, cheese, citrus segments, and other cut-up fruits all work beautifully in grain salads.

## how to cook grains

**pearl barley** *1 part grain to 3 parts liquid*
Boil liquid, add pearl barley, reduce to
a simmer, cover, and cook until fluffy,
35–40 minutes. Drain. Triples in volume.

**wheat berries** *1 part grain to 3½ parts
liquid* Soak wheat berries in liquid
overnight. Bring berries and liquid to
a boil, reduce to a simmer, cover, and
cook until tender, 40–50 minutes.
Drain. Yields same volume.

**farro** *1 part grain to 3 parts liquid*
Bring farro and liquid to a boil, reduce
to a simmer, cover, and cook, stirring
occasionally, until tender, 45–60 minutes.
Drain. Doubles in volume.

**quinoa** *1 part grain to 2 parts liquid*
Boil liquid, add quinoa, reduce to
a simmer, cover, and cook until liquid
is absorbed, 12–15 minutes. Fluff with
a fork. Triples in volume.

**Israeli (pearl) couscous** *1 part grain
to 1¼ parts liquid* Toast couscous in
a little olive oil. Add liquid, cover, and
simmer until couscous is tender and
liquid is absorbed, 10–12 minutes. Let
stand covered for 5 minutes, then fluff
with a fork. Doubles in volume.

**brown rice** *1 part grain to 2 parts liquid
for short grain or 2½ parts liquid for
long grain* Bring grain and liquid to a
boil, reduce heat to low, cover, and cook
until liquid is absorbed, 45–50 minutes.
Short grain doubles in volume, long grain
triples to quadruples in volume.

If you like balsamic vinegar, I encourage you to buy *aceto balsamico tradizionale* from Modena or Reggio Emilia, Italy. It is more expensive than everyday supermarket balsamic because it has been rigorously aged, but you need only a small amount to make a big difference. To make sure I don't waste a drop, I plate the radicchio wedges individually and spoon the liquid from the pan over each serving, rather than present the wedges on a platter. If you opt for a more budget-friendly balsamic here, reduce it first with a little brown sugar to intensify its flavor.

# balsamic-glazed roasted radicchio with walnuts *serves 4–6*

2 heads radicchio, about 10 oz (315 g) total weight

3 tablespoons balsamic vinegar

2 tablespoons olive oil

1 tablespoon walnut oil

1 tablespoon pure maple syrup

2 teaspoons chopped fresh thyme

Sea salt and freshly ground pepper

½ cup (2 oz/60 g) chopped walnuts

Preheat the oven to 400°F (200°C).

Cut each radicchio head in half lengthwise. Trim away most of the core (leave just enough to keep the leaves attached) from each half, then cut each half lengthwise into 3 wedges. Arrange the radicchio wedges in a single layer in a roasting pan.

In a small bowl, whisk together the vinegar, olive oil, walnut oil, and maple syrup. Whisk in the thyme and a pinch each of salt and pepper. Pour the vinegar mixture over the radicchio wedges and turn them to coat evenly.

Roast for 10 minutes. Turn the radicchio and sprinkle the walnuts evenly over the top. Continue to roast until the wedges are tender and the outer leaves are crisped and browned, about 10 minutes longer. Transfer to a serving platter or individual plates and spoon the walnuts and liquid from the roasting pan over the top. Serve hot or at room temperature.

## pack to go

An easy way to transport these same flavors to a party is to make a radicchio slaw: Roast the radicchio (or use it raw), shred it, and toss it with the walnuts. Thin the glaze from the roasting pan with an everyday balsamic vinegar (or if the radicchio is raw, mix the glaze as directed and then thin it) and use it as a dressing. I sometimes add shredded cabbage or carrots to the slaw, as well.

In spring, when it is finally warm enough for an alfresco lunch and asparagus is available at the farmers' market, this is the recipe I make to celebrate. It is also good topped with softly poached eggs: the warm yolks ooze over the tender-crisp spears and create a pleasing contrast with the mustard vinaigrette. Pour a cool, crisp white wine and you have the perfect lunch.

# grilled asparagus with bacon vinaigrette *serves 4–6*

4 slices bacon

2 tablespoons white wine vinegar

1 shallot, finely minced

1 tablespoon Dijon mustard

1 teaspoon chopped fresh thyme

2 tablespoons extra-virgin olive oil, plus more if needed

1 lb (500 g) slender asparagus spears, woody ends snapped off

Sea salt and freshly ground pepper

## make ahead

If I am cooking bacon for breakfast, I fry up enough extra to use in this bacon vinaigrette that night. You can also assemble the vinaigrette and store it, tightly covered in the refrigerator, for up to 4 days. The vinaigrette is versatile, too. It is good tossed with boiled new potatoes or with a butter lettuce and avocado salad.

In a large frying pan, cook the bacon over medium heat until crisp, 7–10 minutes. Transfer to paper towels to drain. Reserve the rendered fat in the pan.

In a small bowl, whisk together the vinegar, shallot, mustard, and thyme. Carefully pour the bacon fat through a fine-mesh sieve into a spouted measuring cup. Slowly whisk the bacon fat into the vinegar mixture until smooth and emulsified. Taste the dressing. If it is too strong, adjust with olive oil, ½ teaspoon at a time.

Prepare a hot fire in a charcoal grill, preheat a gas grill to high, or heat a grill pan over high heat. Pat the asparagus dry and put on a platter or in a baking dish. Drizzle with the 2 tablespoons olive oil and roll the asparagus in the oil until well coated. Season with salt. Arrange the asparagus directly over the heat on the grill rack or place in the pan and cook, turning as needed, until nicely browned in spots on all sides without burning, 6–8 minutes.

Crumble the bacon into small pieces. Arrange the asparagus spears on a platter, pour the dressing over, and scatter the bacon over the top. Top with a few grinds of pepper and serve warm.

Choose medium-size tomatoes that are ripe but firm, so they won't fall apart in the oven. I like the mixture of aromatic vegetables in the rice stuffing, but it's the sweet-tart chewiness of the currants and the crunch of the pine nuts that make this easy side dish special. You don't have to use brown rice here, but it is both tastier and more nutritious than regular white rice.

# roasted stuffed tomatoes *serves 6*

6 red and/or yellow uniformly shaped, ripe but firm tomatoes, preferably with green stems

Sea salt and freshly ground pepper

4 tablespoons (2 fl oz/60 ml) olive oil

¾ cup (4 oz/125 g) finely chopped yellow onion

⅓ cup (2 oz/60 g) finely chopped celery

⅓ cup (2 oz/60 g) peeled and finely chopped carrot

¾ cup (2½ oz/75 g) finely chopped portobello mushrooms

2 cloves garlic, minced

2 tablespoons chopped fresh basil

2 tablespoons chopped fresh flat-leaf parsley

3 cups (15 oz/470 g) cooked brown rice

⅓ cup (1½ oz/45 g) pine nuts, toasted

½ cup (3 oz/90 g) dried currants

**fresh take**

This all-purpose stuffing can be used to fill other vegetables, such as bell peppers, or stuffed into the cavity of fish or chicken.

**dress it up**

When my cherry tomato crop is at full tilt, I like to fill the tomatoes with this stuffing and pass them as hors d'oeuvres.

Preheat the oven to 425°F (220°C). Using a serrated knife, cut a thin slice from the stem end of each tomato—just enough to reveal the inner flesh and seeds and make an opening in the cavity wide enough for spooning. Set the tomato tops aside. Using a spoon, scoop the flesh from the insides of the tomatoes, leaving walls about 1 inch (2.5 cm) thick. Sprinkle the inside of each tomato shell generously with salt and invert the tomatoes onto several thicknesses of paper towels and let drain for about 10 minutes. Meanwhile, discard the seed sacs and chop the tomato flesh.

In a large frying pan, heat 1 tablespoon of the olive oil over medium-high heat. Add the onion and sauté until beginning to soften, about 3 minutes. Add the celery and carrot and sauté until softened, about 3 minutes longer. Stir in the mushrooms and garlic and sauté for 30 seconds longer. Stir in the chopped tomato flesh, the basil, parsley, and rice. Remove from the heat and stir in the pine nuts and currants. Season with salt and pepper.

Arrange the tomato shells, cut side up, in a baking dish just large enough to hold them. Spoon the rice mixture into the tomatoes, dividing it evenly; pack the rice lightly and mound it slightly on top. Replace the reserved tops. Drizzle the tomatoes with the remaining 3 tablespoons olive oil.

Roast until the skins begin to brown and just start to split, about 20 minutes. Let cool slightly to allow the tomatoes to firm up and the juices to redistribute. Serve warm.

## — SUMMER TOMATOES —

I'm a backyard gardener, and I'm able to grow many different types of tomatoes each summer. I usually plant heirloom varieties like Green Zebra and Cherokee Purple, though I also always include tasty Sungolds, a popular hybrid orange cherry tomato. Cut in half and topped with flaky salt, a bite-size tomato is one of the earth's perfect foods.

If you don't have a garden but you live near a farmers' market or a farm that grows tomatoes, chances are you can get your hands on a wide range of tomato varieties. A simple salad of sliced red, pink, orange, yellow, purple, and/or green tomatoes is the ultimate colorful celebration of the season.

Except for plum tomatoes, which are best cooked down into a sauce, when tomato season is peaking (for me that's August), I like to eat the harvest as unadulterated as possible. To prepare for the summer bounty, have good-quality olive oil and flaky sea salt on hand at all times. You never know when the perfect plump tomato might come into your life.

## three ways to make the most out of summer tomatoes

**caprese salad** This classic Italian dish combines fresh tomato slices, basil leaves, and slabs of fresh mozzarella with a drizzle of olive oil and/or balsamic vinegar and a pinch of sea salt. I prefer chunks of tomato with pulled hunks of buffalo mozzarella and ribbons of basil. But if the tomatoes are first-rate, how you present them won't matter.

**pizza** Cut 1 large or 2 medium tomatoes into thin slices. Sprinkle about 1 teaspoon salt over the slices and place on paper towels to drain. Meanwhile, bake a simple pizza (page 131) with a thin layer of melted cheese (a mixture of Parmesan and mozzarella, or only mozzarella). Just as it comes out of the oven, pat the tomato slices dry, arrange them on top of the cheese, and then sprinkle with torn basil leaves. For a richer dish, add a few slices of cured meat, like prosciutto or *lardo*.

**gazpacho** When my tomatoes are starting to look funky but their flavor is still good, I reach for the blender and make gazpacho—a light, cool dinner for a hot summer night. In a blender, combine 6 tomatoes, coarsely chopped; ½ cucumber, peeled, seeded, and coarsely chopped; 1 bell pepper and ½ jalapeño chile, both seeded and chopped; a few garlic cloves; a good pour of extra-virgin olive oil; and 2 tablespoons red wine vinegar and process until smooth. With the motor running, add water in a slow stream until the consistency of the gazpacho is just right. Chill well, then season with salt and freshly ground pepper before serving.

When spring gardens start kicking out bushels of sugar snap peas, it can be hard to keep up. I like this simple preparation in which the uncooked peas are tossed with sesame seeds, ginger, and sesame oil. It is the perfect picnic fare, midday finger food, or a side dish on a warm spring night.

## toasted sesame sugar snap peas *serves 4–6*

2 teaspoons sesame seeds

3 tablespoons Asian sesame oil

½ teaspoon peeled and grated fresh ginger

¾ lb (375 g) sugar snap peas, trimmed

Sea salt

**make it a meal**
Cut the dressed peas into pieces and toss with cooked soba noodles, chopped green onions, and some cooked chicken or tofu, then drizzle with a little soy sauce and enjoy as a hot or cold main dish.

In a small, dry saucepan, toast the sesame seeds over medium heat, keeping them moving in the pan at all times, until just golden, about 1 minute. Be careful as they burn easily. Add the sesame oil and ginger, stir once, and remove from the heat. Continue tilting and rotating the pan for 30 seconds or so to cook the ginger evenly.

Add the peas and toss to coat. Transfer to a serving bowl and season with salt. Serve at room temperature.

When I was a child, my parents often took me to a neighborhood Italian restaurant, where we always started our meal with a finger-food favorite of green beans dipped in garlicky walnut pesto. I still remember the snap of the al dente beans and the bite of the garlic. Now, I make a similar version using toasted almonds and haricots verts. If you can't find these slender French beans, substitute any young, tender beans. Almonds make a crunchier and earthier pesto than the usual pine nuts.

# haricots verts with almond pesto *serves 6–8*

Sea salt

½ lb (250 g) haricots verts or slender green beans, trimmed

1 large clove garlic

1 cup (1 oz/30 g) lightly packed fresh flat-leaf parsley leaves

⅓ cup (3 fl oz/80 ml) extra-virgin olive oil

⅓ cup (2 oz/60 g) blanched almonds, toasted and coarsely chopped

### dress it up

Instead of tossing the beans with the pesto, I sometimes make a crudité platter with the haricots verts and a mixture of other crunchy vegetables, like radishes, fennel, and celery, then serve the almond pesto in a small bowl for dipping.

Have ready a large bowl of ice water. Bring a large saucepan three-fourths full of generously salted water to a boil over high heat. Drop in the beans all at once and cook for 3 minutes. Drain and immediately plunge the beans into ice water. Set aside.

In a food processor or blender, combine the garlic, parsley, and ½ teaspoon salt and process until the parsley is finely chopped. With the machine running, add the olive oil in a slow, steady stream and process until a smooth purée forms. Add the almonds and pulse until finely chopped and the pesto is a uniform coarse purée.

Drain the beans and pat dry. Put them in a large bowl, add the pesto, and toss to coat evenly. Arrange the beans on a serving platter or in a bowl and serve at room temperature.

Cauliflower is a revelation when roasted—sweet, toothsome, and nicely caramelized around the edges. Cutting it into florets is one possible route, but thick slices are even easier to cut and show off the pretty, scalloped silhouette of the head. A topping of fresh mint, cayenne, and crisp bread crumbs contrasts deliciously with the creaminess of the sturdy "steaks." I like to serve this spicy side with simple roast chicken or meats.

# caramelized cauliflower steaks *serves 6–8*

2 heads cauliflower, about 3 lb (1.5 kg) total weight, cored

2 tablespoons olive oil, plus more for brushing

Sea salt and freshly ground pepper

¾ cup (1 oz/30 g) *panko* bread crumbs

¼ cup (¼ oz/7 g) lightly packed fresh mint leaves, finely chopped

⅛ teaspoon cayenne pepper, or to taste

**recipe redux**

I always hope for leftovers with this dish. Mince the caramelized cauliflower, add a little grated Parmesan cheese and a drizzle of olive oil, and it's transformed into a delicious pestolike topping for pasta.

Preheat the oven to 400°F (200°C). Have ready 2 large rimmed baking sheets.

Place 1 head of cauliflower on a cutting board and cut it vertically from top to bottom into slices about ½ inch (12 mm) thick. You should have about 8 intact slices; the rest will fall away in florets. Repeat with the second head of cauliflower.

Brush the cauliflower slices generously on both sides with the olive oil. Sprinkle salt and pepper on both sides. Arrange in a single layer on the baking sheets. Roast for 10 minutes.

Meanwhile, coarsely chop the broken-off cauliflower pieces. You should have about 2½ cups (5 oz/155 g). Place in a bowl and add the bread crumbs, mint, and cayenne. Stir to mix thoroughly. Add the 2 tablespoons olive oil and toss to coat the cauliflower with the bread crumb mixture. Season with salt and pepper.

When the cauliflower slices have roasted for 10 minutes, remove the pans from the oven. Carefully turn the slices and sprinkle the cauliflower evenly with the bread crumb mixture. Return to the oven and bake until the cauliflower is tender and the bread crumbs are golden, about 15 minutes longer. Serve hot.

This simple dish takes advantage of the whole head of broccoli. Even if you think you don't like the more fibrous stems, you will likely be converted by these tender spears with perfectly charred edges and tips. I leave any leaves intact and just strip off the dried or bruised parts of the stem. These attractive little garlic-dotted branches make you want to forget your table manners and pick them up with your fingers. I say, go for it!

# roasted broccoli with red pepper flakes and garlic *serves 4–6*

1½ lb (750 g) broccoli heads, ends trimmed

¼ cup (2 fl oz/60 ml) extra-virgin olive oil

3 tablespoons fresh lemon juice, plus more for serving

3 cloves garlic, minced

Pinch of red pepper flakes

Sea salt

## fresh take

I also like to use Broccolini, a smaller, sweeter, more tender cousin of broccoli, for this dish. Sometimes I add some cheese, too: as soon as the broccoli comes out of the oven, sprinkle it with ⅓ cup (1½ oz/45 g) freshly grated Parmesan cheese and toss to distribute evenly.

Preheat the oven to 400°F (200°C).

Cut the broccoli lengthwise into spears 4–6 inches (10–15 cm) long. Using a vegetable peeler or a sharp paring knife, peel off any dried or bruised skin from the stems.

Arrange the spears in a single layer in a roasting pan. Pour the olive oil over the spears, then sprinkle with the lemon juice, garlic, and red pepper flakes. Toss to coat thoroughly.

Roast, turning once about halfway through the cooking time, until the broccoli is tender and the tips and outer edges are crisp and browned, about 15 minutes. Serve right away with an extra squirt of lemon juice and a few pinches of sea salt.

Tiny pastas are surprisingly simple to dress up for dinner. Here, I use *acini di pepe*—"peppercorns"—but other small shapes, such as *orzo* (barley), *stelline* (stars), or *riso* (rice), can be substituted. Follow the cooking instructions on the package. This is the sort of side dish I like to serve as a bed beneath sliced steak or grilled chicken. It is a good way to use up any extra herbs I might have on hand, too, and is just filling enough with a main course of meat or poultry.

# cheesy acini di pepe with fresh herbs *serves 4–6*

Sea salt and freshly ground pepper

8 oz (250 g) *acini di pepe* pasta (about 1¼ cups)

1½ cups (6 oz/185 g) freshly grated Parmesan cheese

¾ cup (¾ oz/20 g) lightly packed chopped mixed fresh herb leaves such as rosemary, sage, thyme, and/or flat-leaf parsley

**fresh take**

In place of the Parmesan, I sometimes swirl in shredded Taleggio or fontina, both of which offer a little more bite. For a carbonara-style flavor, add crisply cooked diced pancetta or bacon.

Bring a large saucepan three-fourths full of lightly salted water to a boil over high heat. Add the pasta and cook, stirring occasionally, until al dente, about 8 minutes. Drain the pasta thoroughly, reserving 2 tablespoons of the cooking water.

Transfer the pasta to a large serving bowl. Add the reserved cooking water, the cheese, herbs, and pepper to taste and toss to mix and coat well. Serve right away.

This creamy gratin, with its golden brown top, is the kind of comfort food I like to serve next to a steak and a glass of red wine on chilly days. The oval nests of pure white, spear-shaped leaves matched with a good melting cheese are like serving a warm salad and side dish at the same time. It is also an easy recipe to scale down to serve two or scale up to feed a crowd.

# endive gratin *serves 4–6*

3 large heads Belgian endive

2 tablespoons olive oil

¼ teaspoon freshly grated nutmeg

Sea salt and freshly ground pepper

¼ cup (2 fl oz/60 ml) heavy cream

⅓ cup (1½ oz/45 g) finely shredded Gruyère cheese

2 tablespoons coarse dried bread crumbs

1 teaspoon grated lemon zest

Preheat the oven to 400°F (200°C).

Trim only the base of the stem of each endive head, so the leaves will remain attached, then cut each head in half lengthwise. Rub the endives all over with the olive oil and sprinkle with the nutmeg, salt, and pepper. Place, cut side down, in a 12-inch (30-cm) oval gratin dish or similarly sized baking dish.

Roast until golden brown on the bottoms, 7–10 minutes. Remove the dish from the oven and, using tongs or a spatula, gently turn the endives. Pour the cream evenly over the top and sprinkle evenly with the cheese. Return to the oven and bake until tender when pierced with a knife, about 10 minutes longer. Remove the dish from the oven and sprinkle the bread crumbs and lemon zest evenly over the top. Return to the oven and bake until the cheese is bubbly and golden brown and the cream has reduced to a glaze, about 5 minutes.

Serve hot, drizzled with spoonfuls of the creamy glaze from the baking dish.

**fresh take**

Gratins are a simple and delicious way to serve vegetables. In winter, I make heartier versions with cauliflower or potatoes; in spring, I like to use colorful chard or spinach. The basic approach is always the same: roasting the vegetables with a creamy concoction and topping with bread crumbs.

Hearty cannellini beans cooked with rosemary are a staple of the Tuscan table.
I like to take this already satisfying dish a step further and add a handful of
shredded fontina. Cooking unpeeled garlic cloves in the broth and then squeezing
them from their skins into the finished beans is an easy flavor-boosting trick.
This is one of my go-to side dishes for friends and family.

# rosemary white beans with fontina *serves 4–6*

1 rounded cup (7 oz/220g) dried
cannellini beans

3 large cloves garlic, unpeeled

2 sprigs fresh rosemary, plus
1½ teaspoons finely chopped rosemary

2 bay leaves

2 tablespoons extra-virgin olive oil

¼ lb (125 g) fontina cheese, shredded

Sea salt and freshly ground pepper

Pick over the beans and remove any grit, small pebbles, or misshapen beans. Put the beans in
a colander, rinse under cold running water, and let drain thoroughly. Transfer the beans to a bowl
and add tepid water to cover by 1 inch (2.5 cm). Let soak at room temperature for at least 6 hours
or up to overnight.

Drain the beans, rinse, and drain again. Put in a large saucepan and add fresh cold water to cover
by 1 inch (2.5 cm). Add the garlic, rosemary sprigs, bay leaves, and olive oil. Bring to a boil over
high heat, then reduce the heat to maintain a low but steady simmer. Cover partially and cook
until the beans are tender but not mealy, about 45 minutes.

Pour off any excess cooking liquid from the beans. Remove and discard the rosemary sprigs
and bay leaves. (If any rosemary leaves have fallen off the stems during cooking, you can leave
them in the beans.) Squeeze the cooked garlic cloves from their skins into the beans. Stir in
about three-fourths of the cheese and the chopped rosemary and season with salt and pepper.
Serve right away, sprinkling the remaining cheese on top.

## recipe redux

Soaking the beans takes time,
so often, when I make this dish,
I cook a double batch of beans.
With the leftovers, I might make
a white bean dip using the same
ingredients, minus the cheese:
In a food processor, purée the
cooked beans, garlic, and some
chopped rosemary, season with
salt and pepper, and then whirl
in as much of the cooking liquid
as needed to make a smooth,
creamy dip. Serve with pita
wedges or sliced vegetables.

## save time

If you're short on time, use
the quick-soak method: After
picking over and rinsing the
beans, transfer them to a
saucepan and add water to
cover by 1 inch (2.5 cm). Bring
to a boil over high heat and
cook for 2 minutes, then remove
from the heat. Cover and let
soak for 1 hour.

Simple and fast, rich and delicious, mashed—or smashed—potatoes are a classic dish on the dinner table, where they are comfortable sitting alongside meat or fowl or sopping up the juices or sauces of a vegetarian main dish. The smashed style of these potatoes leaves chunks for an appealing texture—and makes preparing them a lot easier than mashing them smooth.

# smashed potatoes *serves 4–6*

1½ lb (750 g) red- or ivory-skinned waxy potatoes, or a mixture, each about 1½ inches (4 cm) in diameter, scrubbed

1 cup (8 oz/250 g) crème fraîche

1 tablespoon chopped fresh thyme, plus sprigs for garnish

Sea salt and freshly ground pepper

Cut the potatoes in half and place in a large saucepan. Add cold water to cover and bring to a boil over high heat. Reduce the heat to low, cover, and simmer until the potatoes are tender when pierced with a fork, about 12 minutes.

Drain the potatoes and return them to the warm pan. Add the crème fraîche and chopped thyme. Mash the potatoes with a potato masher or fork just until they begin to break apart. Season with salt and pepper, garnish with the thyme sprigs, and serve right away.

**fresh take**

You can use any waxy potato for this dish, such as fingerling, Yukon gold, purple, Yellow Finn, Red La Soda, or others you find at the store or farmers' market. Because the potatoes are "smashed" with their skins on, I often use at least two different colors to create an eye-catching dish.

I don't let corn's short season keep me from making this bread year-round. In summer, I slice the kernels off freshly picked ears. The rest of the year, I substitute canned creamed corn. I'm embarrassed to say I almost prefer to use the latter because the bread is moister. More indulgent yet, I sometimes drop a generous spoonful of butter on top of the bread when it comes out of the oven.

# skillet cornbread *serves 6–8*

3 ears corn, husks and silks removed

1 cup (5 oz/155 g) yellow cornmeal

½ cup (2½ oz/75 g) unbleached all-purpose flour

1 tablespoon sugar

1 teaspoon baking soda

½ teaspoon baking powder

½ teaspoon salt

2 large eggs

1½ cups (12 oz/375 g) plain whole-milk yogurt

⅓ cup (3 fl oz/80 ml) corn oil

5 tablespoons (2½ oz/75 g) unsalted butter, at room temperature

Place a 10-inch (25-cm) cast-iron frying pan in the oven and preheat to 425°F (220°C).

Cut the kernels from the ears of corn and coarsely chop the kernels. You should have about 1½ cups (9 oz/280 g). Set aside. In a large bowl, whisk together the cornmeal, flour, sugar, baking soda, baking powder, and salt. Set aside.

In a small bowl, lightly beat the eggs. Stir in the yogurt and oil. Add the wet ingredients to the dry ingredients and stir just until combined; do not overmix; the batter will be lumpy. Stir in the corn kernels.

Remove the frying pan from the oven and add the butter. Swirl the pan until the bottom is evenly coated with the melted butter. Immediately pour the batter into the pan. Return the pan to the oven and reduce the oven temperature to 375°F (190°C). Bake until the bread is a deep golden brown on top and the edges are pulling away from the pan, about 20 minutes.

Serve hot, cut into wedges.

### recipe redux

I never mind having cornbread leftover. I'll toast slices the next morning for breakfast and top them with honey. Or, I cut the bread into cubes and either pack them away in the freezer to use for a stuffing or toast them in the oven and use them as croutons in a salad.

### fresh take

Add a little heat: stir a handful of shredded pepper jack cheese or chopped roasted poblano chiles into the batter.

# Desserts

**Cheese-and-fruit pairings** • Melon with honey-lime drizzle • Pineapple with rum-lime drizzle • Apple-cherry crumble • Rhubarb-ginger crumble **Summer fruit** • Rustic fruit galette • Citrus-herb cookies • Grilled peaches with cardamom cream • Strawberries dressed three ways • Macerated cherries with lemon zabaglione • Buttermilk panna cotta with rhubarb compote Simple vanilla ice cream with roasted grapes • **Ice cream** • Cornmeal cake with dulce de leche • Soft chocolate mini cakes • Layered poached pear tart Chilled nectarine-yogurt pie • **Ice pops** • Chocolate-cherry biscotti with almonds

# — CHEESE-AND-FRUIT PAIRINGS —

There are times when I knock myself out preparing a big dinner for friends, and when it comes time to think about dessert, I don't feel like baking a cake or churning a batch of ice cream. Plus, my guests are usually pretty full by dessert time, so I often opt for a simple combination of cheese and seasonal fruit, rather than a rich, splashy finale. This lighter, more savory approach to dessert works for any meal, but it is especially welcome for large gatherings. Preparing a few platters or cutting boards loaded with fruit and cheese can be more appealing than figuring out how many pies to make or stressing about not having enough ramekins for a dozen servings of *panna cotta*.

Use the time you saved ditching a work-intensive dessert to chat with your local fruit vendor and/or cheesemonger about what pairs well. Let one inform the other: if you find yourself with a bumper crop of figs, you might pair them with a wedge of Stilton. Or, take a fig to the cheese shop and try out some other pairing possibilities.

*Few presentations are more visually inviting than a pile of Parmesan shards alongside wedges of perfectly ripe pear, or little hunks of veined Stilton next to succulent figs. Most such combinations are ideally eaten by hand.*

Except for a combination like fresh ricotta or *fromage blanc* and berries, which is best served in bowls, this is a dessert to serve on platters or boards, with the cheese and fruit arranged informally. Slice or cut the fruit when necessary—pears and apples and some stone fruits; halve figs if large—and break off a few small pieces of cheese to show guests this is a casual course. Few presentations are more visually inviting than a pile of Parmesan shards alongside wedges of perfectly ripe pear, or little hunks of veined Stilton next to succulent figs. Most such combinations are ideally eaten by hand.

Among my favorite combinations are fresh ricotta with blackberries and honeycomb; apples with sharp Cheddar; pears with Parmesan and Port; figs with Stilton and dates; and mozzarella with melon.

This is my favorite way to serve watermelon, lightly doused with a sweet-hot-tart drizzle. Sometimes I mix the watermelon with other melons—here, I have added cantaloupe—or with pineapple. This dish is a good addition to a brunch table or is a refreshing way to finish off a summer barbecue. The cayenne pepper provides a touch of heat, but you can leave it out, if you like. A pinch of sea salt is my secret ingredient: it heightens the sweetness of any melon.

# melon with honey-lime drizzle *serves 4–6*

½ cup (6 oz/185 g) honey

¼ cup (2 fl oz/60 ml) fresh lime juice

⅛ teaspoon cayenne pepper (optional)

1 teaspoon grated lime zest

1 small seedless watermelon, about 6 lb (3 kg), or ½ small seedless watermelon and 1 small cantaloupe, about 3 lb (1.5 kg) each

Pinch of sea salt

2–3 tablespoons torn fresh mint leaves

### fresh take

Try other herbs in place of, or in addition to, the mint, such as tarragon, lemon verbena, basil, and finely chopped rosemary.

To make the drizzle, in a small saucepan over medium-high heat, combine the honey, lime juice, and cayenne pepper, if using. Bring to a boil, then reduce the heat to low and simmer for 3 minutes to allow the flavors to blend. Remove from the heat and let cool until lukewarm. Stir in the lime zest. Let cool to room temperature.

Cut the rind off the watermelon and cut the flesh into small triangular slices or bite-size cubes. If using the cantaloupe, halve and seed it, cut the flesh off the rind, and then cut the flesh into slices. Place in a wide, shallow bowl and drizzle with half of the honey-lime drizzle. Toss gently to coat, then drizzle with the remaining syrup. Sprinkle with the salt and mint and serve.

The rich caramellike, spicy character of dark rum marries deliciously with the natural sweetness of pineapple. I add a generous measure of lime juice and grated lime zest to brighten the flavors, and then finish this simple dessert with delicate ribbons of cooling mint. It is the perfect finale to a summertime supper of chicken and vegetables cooked on the grill.

# pineapple with rum-lime drizzle *serves 4-6*

½ cup (6 fl oz/185 ml) honey

¼ cup (2 fl oz/60 ml) fresh lime juice

3 tablespoons dark rum

1 teaspoon grated lime zest

1 large pineapple

Pinch of fine sea salt

2–3 tablespoons torn fresh mint leaves

## pack to go

This dessert packs neatly for toting to a picnic or potluck. Put the pineapple and drizzle in separate containers, then toss together and sprinkle with the mint and salt just before serving.

To make the drizzle, in a small saucepan over medium-high heat, combine the honey, lime juice, and rum. Bring to a boil, then reduce the heat to low and simmer for 3 minutes to allow the flavors to blend. Remove from the heat and let cool until lukewarm. Stir in the lime zest, then let cool to room temperature.

Cut the crown off the pineapple, then cut off the skin. Cut the pineapple lengthwise into quarters. Trim the core and "the eyes" from each quarter, and cut the quarters into large cubes. Place the cubes in a bowl, pour in the rum-lime drizzle, and toss gently to coat the pineapple thoroughly. Sprinkle with the salt and mint and serve right away.

In fall, as the weather cools, I crave no-fuss desserts that draw on the season's bounty. Here, I tuck tart green apple slices—Newtown Pippin, Granny Smith, Rhode Island Greening, and Baldwin are all good choices—under an oat-flecked golden topping. The piquant dried cherries add a touch of sweetness and color to the filling.

# apple-cherry crumble *serves 6–8*

1¼ cups (6½ oz/200 g) unbleached all-purpose flour

¾ cup (2 oz/60 g) old-fashioned rolled oats

¾ cup (6 oz/185 g) firmly packed light brown sugar

1½ teaspoons grated lemon zest

2 teaspoons ground cinnamon

½ teaspoon freshly grated nutmeg

¼ teaspoon sea salt

6 tablespoons (3 oz/90 g) unsalted butter, cut into small pieces, plus more for greasing

5 tart green apples, cored and sliced

1 tablespoon fresh lemon juice

¾ cup (3 oz/90 g) dried cherries or cranberries

1 cup (8 oz/250 g) granulated sugar

Vanilla ice cream for serving (optional)

In a bowl, stir together 1 cup (5 oz/155 g) of the flour, the oats, brown sugar, lemon zest, cinnamon, nutmeg, and salt. Scatter 4 tablespoons (2 oz/60 g) of the butter over the top and, using your fingers, 2 knives, or a pastry blender, work in the butter until the mixture is crumbly. Set aside. (Mixture can be made up to 2 days ahead and refrigerated, covered.)

Preheat the oven to 350°F (180°C). Lightly butter a shallow 2-qt (2-l) baking dish.

Place the apple slices in a large bowl, sprinkle with the lemon juice, and toss them to coat evenly. Add the cherries, granulated sugar, and the remaining ¼ cup (1½ oz/45 g) flour and toss to combine. Transfer the apple mixture to the prepared baking dish and spread in an even layer. Dot the top with the remaining 2 tablespoons butter. Sprinkle the oat mixture evenly over the fruit.

Bake until the topping is deep gold and the juices are bubbling, about 1 hour. Serve warm or at room temperature, with the vanilla ice cream, if you like.

**fresh take**

Trade out the apples for sliced pears—Bartlett, Anjou, Bosc, and Winter Nellis are all good bakers—and the dried cherries for dried blueberries. You can also serve whipped cream, spiked with a little brandy or pear eau-de-vie, if you like, in place of the ice cream.

**make ahead**

The crumble topping can be made up to 2 days ahead and stored, tightly covered, in the refrigerator.

Whichever fruit is in season, whether it's apples in fall or peaches in summer, I can't resist getting knee deep in it. A crumble is my favorite way to deal with an overflowing fruit bowl, and this is the version I make come spring when tangy rhubarb first appears in the markets.

# rhubarb-ginger crumble *serves 6–8*

6 tablespoons (3 oz/90 g) unsalted butter, cut into ¼-inch (6-mm) cubes, plus more for greasing

1 cup (5 oz/155 g) unbleached all-purpose flour

¾ cup (6 oz/185 g) firmly packed light brown sugar

¾ cup (4 oz/125 g) chopped almonds

⅓ cup (2 oz/60 g) finely chopped crystallized ginger

¼ teaspoon sea salt

2 lb (1 kg) rhubarb, trimmed and cut into ¾-inch (2-cm) pieces (about 6 cups)

1 tablespoon peeled and minced fresh ginger

¾ cup (6 oz/185 g) granulated sugar

Vanilla ice cream for serving (optional)

Preheat the oven to 350°F (180°C). Lightly butter a shallow 2-qt (2-l) baking dish.

In a bowl, stir together the flour and brown sugar. Scatter 4 tablespoons (2 oz/60 g) of the butter over the top and, using your fingers, 2 knives, or a pastry blender, work in the butter until the mixture is crumbly. Add the almonds, crystallized ginger, and salt and toss to combine. Set aside.

In a large bowl, combine the rhubarb, fresh ginger, and granulated sugar and toss to mix well. Transfer the rhubarb mixture to the prepared baking dish and spread in an even layer. Dot with the remaining 2 tablespoons butter. Sprinkle the almond mixture evenly over the fruit.

Bake until the topping is deep gold and the juices are bubbling, about 1 hour. Serve warm or at room temperature, with the vanilla ice cream, if you like.

## fresh take

There are no rules when it comes to crumbles, and I like to vary the flavors and fruit combinations with the seasons. In summer, try nectarines and blueberries or a plum-almond mixture; in fall, combine apples and cherries (page 189).

## dress it up

At my house, vanilla ice cream is pretty much a required topping for any crumble or cobbler. Churn up a homemade batch (page 205), or purchase a top-quality brand at the market.

## make ahead

The crumble topping can be made up to 2 days ahead and stored, tightly covered, in the refrigerator.

## — SUMMER FRUIT —

When I crave something sweet in the summer months, I invariably think of fruit. In the Northeast, that craving begins in May with the first crimson burst of strawberries. June brings cherries. Then, as the weather steadily warms in July and August, apricots, peaches, plums, and other stone fruits appear. Throughout the summer, my raspberry patch produces a steady supply of pink berries, and my fig tree eases the blow of the season's waning by delivering a big crop of sweet, juicy black fruits. As summer ends, the arrival of pear and apple season delivers a soft landing that takes me through the winter.

Of course, nothing is more perfect than a bite of a just-ripe piece of fruit. But when I have more than a few pieces on hand, I often think of ways that I can cook them. A crumble (page 191) and a galette (page 195) are two simple desserts that will put your best summer fruit on a pedestal. These and other baked desserts are also kind to slightly overripe or bruised fruit.

*Nothing is more perfect than a bite of a just-ripe piece of fruit. But when I have more than a few pieces on hand, I often think of ways that I can cook them.*

I like plums with anything almond: chopped almonds, almond extract, and almond paste. Peaches mate deliciously with berries, especially blackberries. Apples and pears figure prominently in my end-of-summer pies, crumbles, and cakes, and I like to pair them with spices like ginger and cardamom. Keep in mind that the sweetness you experience when taking a bite of raw fruit dissipates with cooking, so a little sugar is needed to make sure the dessert won't be too tart or sour. And there's no arguing that summer fruit only gets better with a dollop of whipped cream or a scoop of ice cream.

# rustic fruit galette *serves 6–8*

**for the crust**

1¾ cups (9 oz/280 g) unbleached all-purpose flour, plus more for dusting

2 teaspoons sugar

½ teaspoon salt

¾ cup (6 oz/185 g) cold unsalted butter, cut into ¼-inch (6-mm) cubes

Ice water as needed

**for the filling**

4 tablespoons (2 oz/60 g) sugar

2 tablespoons cornstarch

Pinch of freshly grated nutmeg

1½ lb (750 g) firm but ripe apricots, nectarines, or peaches, or a combination, halved and pitted, and each half cut into 4 wedges

2 tablespoons unsalted butter, cut into ¼-inch (6-mm) cubes

1 tablespoon heavy cream

Whipped cream or crème fraîche for serving (optional)

## pastry lessons

Think of a galette as a relaxed pie—all the crusty and fruity goodness, minus the plate. The crust is folded up in free-form pleats that get golden edges in the oven, hold in the filling, and show off the colorful plumped fruit in the center. As with all pastry making, it's important to keep the dough ingredients cool as you work. The dough is forgiving, and it can be wrapped in a double layer of plastic wrap and frozen for up to 3 months. Thaw it in the refrigerator overnight before using.

## fresh takes

To make an apple-ginger galette, substitute apples for the apricots, cutting them into thin slices. Omit the cornstarch, swap cinnamon for the nutmeg, and add a pinch of ground ginger. The galette may need to cook longer for the fruit to caramelize; if the crust starts to brown too much, cover it with aluminum foil. To make a peach-berry galette, substitute ½ lb (250 g) peaches, cutting them into thin slices, and 2 cups (8 oz/250 g) blackberries, blueberries, or raspberries. Substitute cinnamon for the nutmeg (or use both).

To make the crust, in a food processor, combine the flour, sugar, and salt. Pulse a few times to combine. Scatter the butter pieces over the flour mixture and pulse until the butter is cut into the flour mixture in uniform pieces about the size of peas. Sprinkle the ice water, 1 tablespoon at a time, over the butter-flour mixture and pulse once after each addition. Continue adding water and pulsing until the dough forms small, crumbly lumps, like cottage cheese. Do not overprocess; the dough should not form a ball while still in the processor.

Dump out the dough onto a lightly floured work surface and form into a disk about 1 inch (2.5 cm) thick. Try not to handle it too much. Wrap the disk in plastic wrap and refrigerate until well chilled, at least 30 minutes or up to 2 hours.

To make the filling, in a large bowl, stir together 3 tablespoons of the sugar, the cornstarch, and the nutmeg. Add the apricots and toss to coat evenly.

Position a rack in the lower third of the oven and preheat to 400°F (200°C). Line a baking sheet with parchment paper.

Unwrap the dough disk and place on a lightly floured work surface. Using a floured rolling pin, roll out the dough into a round 13–14 inches (33–35 cm) in diameter. Transfer the dough to the prepared baking sheet. Mound the fruit mixture in the center of the dough round, leaving a 2-inch (5-cm) border uncovered around the edges. Fold the edges up over the filling, pinching pleats as you work. Dot the exposed fruit with the butter. Brush the folded edges with the heavy cream, then sprinkle with the remaining 1 tablespoon sugar.

Bake for 30 minutes. Reduce the oven temperature to 350°F (180°C) and bake until the crust is golden and the juices are bubbling, 10–15 minutes longer. Let cool on the pan on a wire rack for about 5 minutes, then slip the parchment paper with the galette off the baking sheet onto the wire rack and let cool completely.

Cut into wedges and serve topped with a dollop of whipped cream, if you like.

This surprising combination of aromatic herbs, tart citrus, and buttery, sweet dough satisfies even the fussiest cookie aficionado. I developed the recipe using orange zest and thyme leaves, but you can use the basic dough to experiment with other flavors to come up with your own signature cookies.

# citrus-herb cookies *makes about 3 dozen*

1 cup (8 oz/250 g) unsalted butter, at room temperature

⅔ cup (5 oz/155 g) granulated sugar

⅛ teaspoon sea salt

1 large egg

2 tablespoons grated orange zest

2 teaspoons very finely chopped fresh thyme leaves

6–8 fresh mint leaves very finely sliced

2½ cups (12½ oz/390 g) unbleached all-purpose flour

Raw or turbinado sugar for sprinkling

In a bowl, combine the butter, granulated sugar, and salt. Using a wooden spoon or an electric mixer set on medium speed, beat until smooth. Add the egg, orange zest, thyme, and mint and beat until well mixed. Reduce the speed to low and gradually add the flour in 3 batches, beating after each addition, until combined. Divide the dough in half and shape each portion into a log about 1½ inches (4 cm) in diameter. Wrap the logs tightly in plastic wrap and refrigerate until well chilled, at least 1 hour or up to overnight.

Preheat the oven to 350°F (180°C) and position the rack in the middle level. Line 2 large rimmed baking sheets with parchment paper or silicone baking mats.

Remove the dough logs from the refrigerator. For round cookies, roll the plastic-wrapped logs on a work surface (like rolling a rolling pin) to smooth the sides, keeping the diameter uniform. For square cookies, using your hands, tap each wrapped log on 4 sides against the work surface to flatten the sides evenly. Unwrap the logs and, using a sharp knife, cut the logs crosswise into slices about ¼ inch (6 mm) thick.

Arrange the cookies on the prepared baking sheets. Sprinkle each cookie with a pinch of raw sugar. Bake the cookies, rotating the sheets front to back after about 5 minutes, until light golden brown, about 10 minutes.

Let the cookies cool on the pans on wire racks for a few minutes, then use a metal spatula to transfer the cookies to wire racks and let cool completely. Store in an airtight container at room temperature for up to 2 days.

## fresh take

Lemon and rosemary, lime and mint, grapefruit and sage—be daring with how you flavor the cookies, choosing different pairs of citrus and herbs.

## perfect partner

In the summer months, I serve these cookies with a pitcher of iced tea. In winter, I make espresso or hot tea. For an adults-only affair, I offer brandy, sherry, or *vin santo*.

## save time

The dough can be stored overnight in the refrigerator, so you can make the dough one night and bake the cookies the next night.

Stone fruit seared on a hot grill and topped with billowy whipped cream is one of the best ways to end a summer meal—and one of the easiest endings to make, too. If you don't want to fire up the grill, roast the peaches in the oven instead. You can trade out the cardamom for another spice, such as cinnamon, or you can replace the spice in the cream with a splash of vanilla or brandy.

# grilled peaches with cardamom cream *serves 4–6*

3 tablespoons honey

1 tablespoon brandy or fruit-based liqueur

½ teaspoon ground cardamom

4 firm but ripe peaches, halved and pitted

Olive oil for brushing

½ cup (4 fl oz/125 ml) cold heavy cream

In a bowl, combine the honey, brandy, and ¼ teaspoon of the cardamom. Whisk briskly to loosen the honey and mix well. Add the peach halves and toss gently to coat. Cover and set aside at room temperature until ready to cook.

Prepare a hot fire in a charcoal grill, preheat a gas grill to high, or heat a grill pan over high heat. Brush the grill rack or pan with olive oil.

Meanwhile, in a chilled metal or glass bowl, using an electric mixer set on medium speed, beat the cream until soft peaks form, about 4 minutes. Add the remaining ¼ teaspoon cardamom and beat until fluffy, stiff peaks form, 1–2 minutes longer. Cover and refrigerate until ready to serve.

Using tongs, remove the peach halves from the honey mixture and arrange, cut side down, on the grill rack or pan, reserving the remaining honey mixture. Cook the peach halves until tender and nicely grill marked, 3–4 minutes.

Transfer the peaches to a platter or individual plates or bowls and let cool slightly. Serve warm, topped with the cardamom whipped cream and drizzled with the reserved honey mixture.

## fresh take

Other fruits, such as nectarines, apricots, and pluots, are good candidates for this summertime grilled dessert, too. You can also grill the fruits, minus the honey-brandy dunk, and then chop them and add them to a green salad. Arugula is good match for the caramelized flavors of the fruit.

## change the method

You can also roast the peaches: Preheat the oven to 400°F (200°C). Arrange the peaches, cut side up, in a baking dish and roast until tender, lightly browned, and beginning to caramelize, 10–20 minutes, depending on how ripe the peaches are.

When local strawberries are bursting with flavor, use this recipe. You don't need to do a thing to the berries except bow down to their sweetness. Instead, you whip up three sauces—thickened spiced wine, creamy chocolate, and liquor-spiked cream—and let your guests choose the one they want. If they will be dipping the berries, leave the stems attached to use as handles.

# strawberries dressed three ways *serves 4–6*

for the spiced wine sauce

2 cups (16 fl oz/500 ml) fruity red wine

1 whole star anise

5 whole peppercorns

for the chocolate sauce

½ cup (4 fl oz/125 ml) heavy cream

¼ cup (2 oz/60 g) granulated sugar

1 tablespoon unsalted butter

¼ teaspoon sea salt

6 oz (185 g) bittersweet chocolate, finely chopped

½ teaspoon pure vanilla extract

for the spiked whipped cream

½ cup (4 fl oz/125 ml) heavy cream

¼ cup (1 oz/30 g) confectioners' sugar

1 tablespoon rum, Cointreau, brandy, or liquor of choice

2 pt (1 lb/500 g) ripe strawberries, stemmed if not dipping

## pack to go

To bring this dessert on the road, pack the berries in one big container, and each sauce in its own container, and assemble the platter when ready to serve.

To make the wine sauce, in a small saucepan, combine the wine, star anise, and peppercorns and bring to a boil over medium heat. Reduce the heat to low and simmer gently until reduced by half, about 30 minutes. Strain the sauce through a fine-mesh sieve into a small serving bowl. (The wine sauce can be served warm, cold, or at room temperature. To reheat, warm gently in a small saucepan.)

To make the chocolate sauce, in a saucepan over medium heat, combine the cream, granulated sugar, butter, and salt and cook, stirring constantly, until the sugar dissolves and bubbles form around the edges of the pan. Remove the pan from the heat. Add the chocolate and stir until the chocolate is melted and the sauce is smooth. Stir in the vanilla. Transfer to a small serving bowl. (The chocolate sauce can be served warm, cold, or at room temperature. To reheat, pour into a heatproof bowl, and heat over, not touching, simmering water in a saucepan.)

To make the whipped cream, in a chilled metal or glass bowl, using an electric mixer set on medium speed, beat the cream until foamy. Sprinkle in the confectioners' sugar and the liquor and continue beating until soft peaks form, 4–5 minutes. Transfer to a small serving bowl, or cover and refrigerate until ready to serve.

Serve the strawberries, stems intact, on a platter and pass with the sauces for dipping. Or, remove the stems and spoon strawberries into individual bowls; pass the sauces for drizzling.

Zabaglione, a kind of Italian custard, is made by beating together egg yolks, sugar, and wine over simmering water until the mixture thickens and increases in volume. A sweet Marsala is traditional, though you can use any wine you like. I add lemon juice to temper the richness, but other citrus juice would be good, too. This frothy, fluffy custard is a versatile topping: spoon it over brownies, fruit, cake, or pie.

# macerated cherries with lemon zabaglione *serves 4–6*

**for the macerated cherries**

⅔ cup (5 fl oz/160 ml) dry white wine

2 tablespoons sugar

Grated zest of 1 lemon

1 lb (500 g) fresh cherries, pitted

**for the zabaglione**

4 large egg yolks

¼ cup (2 fl oz/60 ml) Marsala, port, sherry, or Madeira

¼ cup (2 oz/60 g) sugar

2 tablespoons fresh lemon juice

**make ahead**

The cherries, as noted in the recipe, can macerate overnight. The zabaglione can also be made in advance and served cold. Prepare as directed, then let cool, cover, and refrigerate for up to 3 days.

To make the macerated cherries, in a saucepan, combine the wine, ¼ cup (2 fl oz/60 ml) water, and the sugar and bring to a boil over medium-high heat, stirring to dissolve the sugar. Reduce the heat to low and simmer, stirring occasionally, until reduced to a thick syrup, about 15 minutes. Add the lemon zest and the cherries and stir over low heat for 2 minutes. Remove the cherries from the heat and let cool to room temperature. Cover and macerate in the refrigerator for at least 3 hours or up to overnight.

To make the zabaglione, in a stainless-steel bowl, whisk together the egg yolks, Marsala, and sugar. Place the bowl over (not touching) barely simmering water in a saucepan. Whisk the yolk mixture vigorously until warm, frothy, and thick, about 8 minutes, taking care not to let the mixture get hot. If it starts to feel too warm (warmer than body temperature is a good gauge), lift the bowl away from the hot water and continue whisking until it cools slightly, then return to the heat. Repeat as needed until the zabaglione is ready. The finished sauce should be the consistency of lightly whipped cream. Stir in the lemon juice.

To serve, drain the cherries (reserve the macerating liquid for another use). Spoon the cherries into a serving bowl or individual bowls and scoop the warm zabaglione on top. Serve right away.

This Italian dessert neatly combines simplicity and elegance. Somewhere between a custard and a gelled dessert, *panna cotta* is the perfect make-ahead dish: it takes little effort to assemble but needs at least 4 hours to set. Here, tart rhubarb is flavored with balsamic vinegar, resulting in a bright-tasting, syrupy, crimson compote that contrasts perfectly with the creamy white *panna cotta*.

# buttermilk panna cotta with **rhubarb compote** *serves 6*

2 cups (16 fl oz/500 ml) buttermilk

1 teaspoon unflavored gelatin

⅔ cup (5 oz/155 g) granulated sugar

1½ cups (12 fl oz/375 ml) half-and-half

for the rhubarb compote

1½ lb (750 g) rhubarb, trimmed and cut into ¾-inch (2-cm) pieces

¾ cup (6 oz/185 g) firmly packed light brown sugar

2 tablespoons balsamic vinegar

½ teaspoon ground cinnamon

¼ teaspoon freshly grated nutmeg

¼ teaspoon sea salt

Fresh mint sprigs for garnish

**perfect partner**

I like to serve *panna cotta* with a clear-flavored hot drink, such as espresso or tisane (page 34) to cut through the buttery richness.

**fresh take**

You can use other fruits, or a combination of favorites, to make the compote. Sometimes I mix strawberries with the rhubarb, and in late summer I like using stone fruits, like plums, peaches, or nectarines.

Pour 1 cup (8 fl oz/250 ml) of the buttermilk into a heatproof bowl. Sprinkle the gelatin over the top and let soften for 3–5 minutes.

In a saucepan, combine the granulated sugar and half-and-half over medium heat and whisk until the sugar dissolves. Bring to a simmer, then pour the hot mixture over the gelatin mixture. Whisk until the gelatin is dissolved. Stir in the remaining 1 cup (8 fl oz/250 ml) buttermilk.

Strain the buttermilk mixture through a fine-mesh sieve into a large glass measuring pitcher, then divide it evenly among six ¾-cup (6 fl–oz/180-ml) ramekins. Cover and refrigerate until completely set, at least 4 hours or up to 24 hours.

Preheat the oven to 350°F (180°C).

To make the compote, in a baking dish, combine the rhubarb, brown sugar, vinegar, cinnamon, nutmeg, and salt and toss to combine. Spread the mixture in an even layer and roast, stirring several times, just until the rhubarb is very soft when pierced, about 25 minutes. Let cool, then cover and refrigerate until ready to serve.

To unmold each ramekin, run a thin-bladed knife around the inside edge to loosen the *panna cotta*, then invert it onto an individual plate. Top with the compote, garnish with the mint, and serve.

# simple vanilla ice cream with roasted grapes *serves 4–6*

2 cups (16 fl oz/500 ml) heavy cream

1 cup (8 fl oz/250 ml) whole milk

⅔ cup (5 oz/155 g) sugar

Pinch of sea salt

1 vanilla bean, split in half lengthwise, plus 1 teaspoon pure vanilla extract if using the quick method

1½ teaspoons pure vanilla extract, if using the quicker method

for the roasted grapes

½ lb (250 g) red seedless grapes

2 teaspoons olive oil

1 tablespoon sugar

⅛ teaspoon ground cinnamon

¼ cup (2 fl oz/60 ml) fruity red wine

*To make the ice cream by the quick method,* in a saucepan, combine 1 cup (8 fl oz/250 ml) of the cream, ½ cup (4 fl oz/125 ml) of the milk, the sugar, and the salt and stir to mix. Using the tip of a paring knife, scrape in the vanilla seeds, then drop in the pod. Place over medium-low heat and cook, stirring constantly, until the sugar dissolves and bubbles form around the edges of the pan.

Remove from the heat and add the remaining 1 cup (8 fl oz/250 ml) cream and ½ cup (4 fl oz/125 ml) milk and the 1 teaspoon vanilla extract. Cover and refrigerate until thoroughly chilled, about 2 hours. Before churning, remove the vanilla pod (it can be gently cleaned and put into a canister of sugar to flavor it) and stir the ice cream base. Freeze in an ice-cream maker according to the manufacturer's instructions, then transfer to an airtight container and place in the freezer until ready to serve.

*To make the ice cream by the quicker method,* in a bowl, combine the cream, milk, sugar, salt, and 1½ teaspoons vanilla and stir briskly until the sugar dissolves, about 1 minute. Freeze in an ice-cream maker according to the manufacturer's instructions.

Preheat the oven to 400°F (200°C).

To make the roasted grapes, place the grapes in a single layer in a baking dish. Drizzle with the olive oil, sprinkle with the sugar and cinnamon, and shake the dish or toss gently to distribute the ingredients and coat the grapes. Roast, shaking the dish occasionally, until the grapes begin to break apart, about 20 minutes. Carefully pour in the wine, tilting the dish to swish the wine into all the corners. Raise the oven temperature to 500°F (260°C) and roast until the grapes look slightly deflated, about 10 minutes longer.

To serve, scoop the ice cream into individual bowls and top with the warm grapes. Drizzle with the juice in the baking dish.

## save time

If you decide to make ice cream, you don't need to set aside a whole afternoon. Skip making the classic custard, which takes time and constant attention. Instead, opt for either the quick or quicker method I suggest here. The quick method infuses the hot cream-milk mixture with a vanilla bean and then chills the mixture before churning. The quicker method just stirs together all the ingredients and pours the mixture into the ice-cream maker. Either way, your ice cream will have a rich, creamy, custardlike flavor.

## fresh take

You can make other kinds of fruit "sundaes," too. Try roasting cherries, apricots, or figs in place of the grapes.

## make ahead

The ice cream can be made and frozen up to 1 week ahead of time. The grapes will keep, tightly covered in the refrigerator, for up to 3 days. Reheat gently over low heat.

# — ICE CREAM —

I am always ready to churn up a batch of ice cream, and I don't even have the sweetest tooth in our house. Even the process of making it is a form of indulgence, so by the time it's ready to eat, just a few bites often satisfy me—though it's hard not to dip in for more. Making it is easy, too. I have included two quick methods on page 205; here is a slower method that calls for preparing a custard base. The amount of sugar you will need depends on the flavor of the ice cream and your personal taste. This recipe is good if you are making vanilla or using one of the sweeter fruits, such as peaches or strawberries. Taste the custard before you chill it, and if it needs more sugar, add it then.

## flavor variations

**vanilla**  Use a vanilla bean rather than pure vanilla extract, though extract will still yield a good flavor. If using extract, add 1 teaspoon, stirring it into the finished base. If using a vanilla bean, slit it lengthwise and scrape the seeds into the milk mixture before you heat it, then add the spent pod. Remove the pod before you add the hot milk mixture to the egg mixture.

**chocolate**  Add 3 tablespoons unsweetened cocoa powder to the milk mixture as it heats, whisking to dissolve. When hot, whisk in 4 oz (125 g) bittersweet chocolate, chopped. Increase the salt by a pinch or two to bring out the chocolate flavor.

**coffee and tea**  For coffee ice cream, add about ¼ cup (1¾ oz/50 g) ground dark-roast coffee (I use decaf) to the milk only (no cream) and heat—"brew"—until small bubbles appear around the edges of the pan. Let cool, cover, and steep in the refrigerator for a few hours. Then proceed as directed, adding the cream and straining the base just before chilling. For most tea ice creams, use 3–4 tablespoons loose-leaf tea and "brew" as for the coffee method. For green tea ice cream, add 1 tablespoon *matcha* (powdered green tea) to the milk and whisk or process in a blender to dissolve completely. Add the now-green milk to the cream and proceed with the custard method.

**fruit**  For berries, stone fruits, apples, and pears, add 1 cup fruit purée to the cooked base before you chill it. For stone fruits (peeled or unpeeled) and berries, purée the fruit in a food processor. For apples and pears, simmer the fruit in a little water or juice and a few spoonfuls of sugar, then purée. For citrus, use 1–2 tablespoons grated zest and ½ cup (4 fl oz/125 ml) fresh juice. Stir half the zest into the milk mixture before you heat it, then stir the remaining zest and the juice into the custard before you chill it. Keep in mind that tarter fruits will require more sugar in the base or dissolved in the purée.

**herbs**  Basil, rosemary, lavender, thyme, and mint are all good choices. The amount used depends on how strong the herb is. I add about 1 cup (1½ oz/45 g) coarsely chopped fresh basil or mint, a few sprigs rosemary or thyme, or a handful of lavender buds to the milk mixture before I heat it, then I strain the custard before chilling it.

**spices**  I add the spice to the milk mixture before I heat it, then I strain the custard before chilling. Some of my favorites are 1 or 2 whole star anise pods, ½ teaspoon whole cloves or whole allspice, 5 or 6 cardamom pods, 2 or 3 cinnamon sticks, or 1 small chunk of nutmeg.

**alcoholic beverages**  Add 3–4 tablespoons of the beverage to the custard before chilling. If using beverages with a low-alcohol content, such as beer or wine, use up to 1 cup (8 fl oz/250 ml). Note that because of the alcohol, the ice cream won't freeze as hard.

## basic custard ice cream base

1½ cups (12 fl oz/375 ml) heavy cream
1½ cups (12 fl oz/375 ml) whole milk
5 large egg yolks
⅔ cup (5 oz/155 g) sugar
⅛ teaspoon salt
*makes about 1 qt (1 l) ice cream*

Select a flavor from the suggestions
(opposite) and add it as directed.
Set a fine-mesh sieve over a medium
bowl, and prepare an ice bath in
a large bowl.

In a 2-qt (2-l) or larger, heavy-bottomed
saucepan, combine the cream and milk
and heat over medium heat until small
bubbles appear around the edges
of the pan, about 5 minutes. Remove
from the heat.

In a medium bowl, whisk together the egg
yolks, sugar, and salt until thick and pale
yellow, about 1 minute. Whisking constantly,
slowly pour in about half of the hot milk
mixture. Then slowly pour the egg mixture
back into the pan with the remaining milk
mixture, whisking as you pour. Simmer
over medium-low heat, stirring constantly
with a wooden spoon in an S motion and
scraping the bottom of the pan as you
stir, until the mixture coats the back of
the spoon and registers 170°F (77°C) on
an instant-read thermometer, 5–8 minutes.

Pour the mixture through the sieve into
the medium bowl, then set the bowl
in the ice bath. Let cool, stirring
occasionally, to room temperature,
10–15 minutes. Cover and refrigerate
until well chilled.

Freeze the custard in an ice-cream
maker according to the manufacturer's
instructions. Pack into a freezer-safe
container to harden further before
serving, if desired.

# cornmeal cake with dulce de leche *serves 8–10*

*for the dulce de leche*

4 cups (32 fl oz/1 l) whole milk

1 cup (8 oz/250 g) sugar

1 cinnamon stick

1 teaspoon pure vanilla extract

¼ teaspoon sea salt

½ teaspoon baking soda dissolved in 1 tablespoon water

Unsalted butter for greasing

1¼ cups (6½ oz/200 g) unbleached all-purpose flour

1 cup (8 oz/250 g) sugar

⅔ cup (3½ oz/105 g) yellow cornmeal

2 teaspoons baking powder

1 teaspoon sea salt

¼ teaspoon ground cinnamon

3 large eggs

¾ cup (6 oz/185 g) sour cream

¼ cup (2 fl oz/60 ml) olive oil

½ teaspoon pure vanilla extract

To make the *dulce de leche,* in a large, heavy-bottomed saucepan, combine the milk, sugar, cinnamon stick, vanilla, and salt. Bring to a simmer over medium heat, stirring to dissolve the sugar. Remove from the heat and stir in the baking soda mixture. Whisk aggressively while the sauce froths up; it will soon settle down. Return the pan to the stove top and, with the heat at its lowest setting, continue to cook, barely simmering, until the sauce reduces to about 1 cup (8 fl oz/250 ml) and is deep brown, 1–2 hours. Remove from the heat and let cool slightly.

Preheat the oven to 350°F (180°C).

Grease an 8-inch (20-cm) round cake pan with butter. Line the bottom of the pan with parchment paper, and grease the top of the paper with more butter.

In a large bowl, whisk together the flour, sugar, cornmeal, baking powder, salt, and cinnamon.

In another large bowl, whisk together the eggs, sour cream, olive oil, and vanilla. Slowly add the dry ingredients to the egg mixture, stirring just until combined; do not overmix.

Scrape the batter into the prepared pan and smooth the top. Bake until the cake starts to pull away from the sides of the pan and a toothpick inserted into the center comes out clean, about 30 minutes. Let cool in the pan on a wire rack for 10 minutes, then run a thin-bladed knife around the edges of the pan to loosen the cake and invert it onto a plate. Peel away the parchment paper, then reinvert the cake onto a serving plate.

Poke the cake all over with a skewer. Slowly and evenly pour about half of the warm *dulce de leche* over the top and allow it to penetrate for a few minutes. Cut the cake into wedges and serve. Place the remaining sauce in a small pitcher and pass at the table.

## perfect partner

This cake starts as a basic cornbread, but then it's given a sweet soaking in the milky caramel treat from Mexico called *dulce de leche*—a little alchemy that yields dessert gold. Accompany it with strongly brewed dark-roast coffee or with espresso to balance the sweetness.

## save time

You can buy cans or jars of *dulce de leche,* including *cajeta,* the more complexly flavored goat's milk version, in many Mexican groceries. But when I have the time, I like to make my own. Be sure to use whole milk, or the *dulce de leche* won't be rich enough.

## make ahead

The *dulce de leche* sauce will keep, tightly covered, in the refrigerator, for up to 1 month. Gently reheat it over low heat or in a microwave oven.

Dinner guests are always thrilled when you serve them their own little warm chocolate cake. The molten mouthfuls never cease to bring smiles and praise. While not supersweet, my version has a deep chocolate flavor and is rich enough to share. I leave room on my palate for a dollop of whipped cream or other cool topping. The success of these cakes depends on two things: the best-quality chocolate and not overcooking them. You want the centers to be almost runny.

# soft chocolate mini cakes *serves 6*

5 tablespoons (2½ oz/75 g) unsalted butter, cut into small cubes, plus more for greasing

8 oz (250 g) bittersweet chocolate, chopped

½ cup (4 oz/125 g) sugar

2 large eggs

1½ teaspoons pure vanilla extract

Pinch of sea salt

¼ cup (1½ oz/45 g) unbleached all-purpose flour

Whipped cream, crème fraîche, or vanilla ice cream for serving (optional)

Position a rack on the lowest level in the oven and preheat to 400°F (200°C). Lightly butter six ½-cup (4 fl–oz/125-g) ramekins.

Put the butter and chocolate in a heatproof bowl and place over (not touching) simmering water in a saucepan. Heat until melted, then stir until smooth. Remove from the heat and let cool slightly.

Meanwhile, in a bowl, combine the sugar, eggs, vanilla, and salt. Using an electric mixer set on high speed, beat until thickened, about 3 minutes. Reduce the speed to low. Gradually sprinkle the flour over the batter and continue beating just until combined. Using a spatula, fold the egg mixture into the cooled chocolate mixture until combined.

Divide the batter among the prepared ramekins. Place the ramekins on a rimmed baking sheet and bake until the tops are puffed and dry and a wooden skewer inserted in the center comes out with some soft batter clinging to it, about 10 minutes.

Serve the cakes hot, in the ramekins, or inverted onto individual plates (right). Top with a dollop of whipped cream, if you like.

**dress it up**

These small, dense chocolate cakes look especially beautiful when served unmolded. Line the bottom of each ramekin with a parchment-paper round, then pour in the batter. (This lining step is painstaking, but the cakes will unmold more easily.) Bake as directed, then remove from the oven. Immediately grasp a ramekin with a pot holder or thick towel, run a thin-bladed knife around the inside edge to loosen the cake, and invert the cake onto a small plate or into a small bowl. Peel off the parchment and serve.

Store-bought sheets of frozen puff pastry open up a whole world of easy-to-make sweet and savory recipes for everything from fancy appetizers to crowd-pleasing desserts. Here, pears are poached in red wine and spices and then layered with rectangles of puff pastry. The result is a patisserie-worthy tart that will have your guests applauding your dessert skills.

# layered poached pear tart *serves 6–8*

2 firm but ripe pears such as Bosc or Comice

1 bottle (24 fl oz/750 ml) dry red wine

½ cup (4 oz/125 g) granulated sugar

1 slice fresh ginger, ¼ inch (6 mm) thick, peeled and cut into a few chunks

5 cardamom pods

for the filling

⅓ cup (3 oz/90 g) granulated sugar

4 tablespoons (2 oz/60 g) unsalted butter, at room temperature

Pinch of sea salt

1 large egg

1 teaspoon pure almond extract

3 tablespoons unbleached all-purpose flour

Unbleached all-purpose flour for dusting

1 sheet (8 oz/250 g) puff pastry, thawed according to package directions

1 large egg, beaten

1 teaspoon turbinado or Demerara sugar

Vanilla ice cream for serving (optional)

**save time**

If you're short on time, skip the pear poaching and use slightly soft—that is, ripe but not mushy—pears tossed with a bit of honey.

**perfect partner**

I like to serve this pretty pear tart with a glass of Port or other after-dinner drink.

Peel, quarter, and core the pears. In a large saucepan, combine the wine, granulated sugar, ginger, and cardamom and bring to a gentle boil over medium-high heat. Add the pears, nudge with a spoon to submerge them in the poaching liquid, and reduce the heat to maintain a gentle simmer.

Cut a circle of parchment paper, slightly smaller than the circumference of the pan, and cut a ½-inch (12-mm) hole in the center to vent the steam. Place the paper round in the pan on top of the pears and poaching liquid. Cook, occasionally lifting the paper and turning the pears gently, until tender, about 30 minutes. Using a slotted spoon, transfer the pears to a plate and let cool. When cool, slice the pear quarters lengthwise into thin slices about ¼ inch (6 mm) thick.

Discard the paper. Raise the heat to medium and simmer the poaching liquid until reduced to a thick syrup, 20–30 minutes. Remove from the heat and let cool to room temperature. Discard the ginger pieces and cardamom pods. Set the syrup aside.

Preheat the oven to 375°F (190°C). Line 2 rimmed baking sheets with parchment paper.

To make the filling, in a bowl, combine the granulated sugar, butter, and salt. Using a wooden spoon, beat until fluffy. Add the egg and almond extract and beat until well combined. Add the flour and beat just until incorporated. Set aside.

On a lightly floured work surface, using a floured rolling pin, roll out the puff pastry into a 9-by-12-inch (23-by-33-cm) rectangle about ¼ inch (6 mm) thick. Dust the rectangle lightly on both sides with flour. Using a sharp knife or a pizza wheel, cut the rectangle in half crosswise, and then cut each half in half lengthwise to make 4 equal smaller rectangles. Roll out each layer into a larger rectangle about 8 by 10 inches (20 by 25 cm) and ⅛ inch (3 mm) thick.

Stack 3 of the 4 pastry rectangles on a prepared baking sheet, placing a sheet of parchment between each layer. Refrigerate until ready to use.

Place the remaining pastry rectangle on the second prepared baking sheet. Using a pastry brush dipped in the beaten egg, paint a 1-inch (2.5-cm) border around the dough. Spread about 2 tablespoons of the filling across the surface, leaving the egg-wash border around the edges uncovered. Arrange one-third of the sliced pears, slightly overlapping, on top of the filling, again leaving the border uncovered. Remove 1 of the pastry rectangles from the refrigerator and place gently on top of the pears. Repeat the process, painting the egg-wash border, spreading another 2 tablespoons of the filling to within 1 inch of the edge, and topping with pear slices. Repeat with the third pastry rectangle, more filling, and the remaining pears, then place the remaining pastry rectangle on top. (You may have a little filling leftover.)

Using your thumb, press firmly around the edges to seal the pastry layers. Using the sharp knife or pizza wheel dipped in flour, trim the edges so they are even. Brush the remaining egg over the top of the tart. With the tip of a paring knife, cut a few steam vents into the top, then sprinkle with the turbinado sugar.

Bake until the crust is shiny with deep golden brown areas, about 30 minutes. (The filling may spill out the sides a little.) Let cool slightly on the pan on a wire rack. When the tart is cool enough to handle, gently peel the parchment paper off the bottom. To serve, cut crosswise into slices. Spoon a pool of the poaching syrup onto each plate, place a warm tart slice on the syrup, and top the tart slice with a scoop of vanilla ice cream, if desired.

# chilled nectarine-yogurt pie *serves 8–10*

for the crust

½ cup (2½ oz/75 g) finely chopped whole raw almonds

1⅓ cups (4 oz/125 g) graham cracker crumbs

2 tablespoons firmly packed light brown sugar

½ teaspoon salt

⅓ cup (3 oz/90 g) unsalted butter, melted

for the filling

1 tablespoon (1 package) unflavored gelatin

1¼ cups (10 oz/315 g) plain whole-milk yogurt

¼ cup (3 oz/90 g) honey

2 teaspoons pure almond extract

1 lb (500 g) firm but ripe nectarines, pitted and finely chopped

¾ cup (6 fl oz/180 ml) heavy cream

Thinly sliced nectarines and/or blueberries for garnish

Small fresh mint leaves for garnish

### when to serve

Folding fruit into honey-sweetened yogurt yields a pie filling that is cool and tangy—a perfect dessert for a hot summer night. Topping the filling with more fruit makes the pie pretty enough to tote to a potluck.

### fresh take

I like the combination of stone fruit and almonds, so here I added ground almonds to a classic graham cracker crust and a splash of almond extract to the filling. If you like, substitute apricots, peaches, or cherries for the nectarines.

Preheat the oven to 350°F (180°C).

To make the crust, in a food processor, combine the almonds, graham cracker crumbs, brown sugar, and salt. Pulse just until the nuts and cracker crumbs are finely and uniformly ground. Be careful not to overprocess or the almonds will turn pasty. Pour in the melted butter and pulse just to combine. Press the crumb mixture evenly onto the bottom and sides of a 9-inch (23-cm) pie dish. Bake until lightly browned and crisp, 8–10 minutes. Let cool completely on a wire rack, about 30 minutes.

Meanwhile, make the filling. Pour 3 tablespoons water into a small heatproof bowl and sprinkle the gelatin over the top. Let soften for 3–5 minutes.

In a medium bowl, whisk together the yogurt, honey, and almond extract. Gently stir in the chopped nectarines. Set aside.

Place the bowl holding the softened gelatin over (not touching) simmering water in a small saucepan and stir until the gelatin dissolves. Stir the gelatin mixture into the yogurt mixture.

Pour the cream into a chilled bowl. Using an electric mixer set on medium speed, beat the cream until soft peaks form. Using a spatula, gently fold the whipped cream into the yogurt mixture until no streaks remain. Pour the filling into the cooled pie crust and refrigerate until well chilled and set, at least 1 hour or up to 3 hours.

When ready to serve, arrange the nectarine slices and/or blueberries in an attractive pattern on top. Garnish with the mint, cut into wedges, and serve cold.

# — ICE POPS —

Ice pops are enjoying a renaissance: in many cities, you'll find ice pops carts on the streets selling über-trendy flavors to hipsters. Restaurants—some of them upscale—are featuring the cold treats on their dessert menus.

Meanwhile, many of us home cooks have never lost our childhood affection for ice pops. I've been whizzing up flavors—some kid-friendly, some not so much—for most of my life. With a child in the house who has an almost sugar-free diet, I have a new reason to experiment with ice pops. Unlike ice cream, they are easy to make with little or no added sugar. My little girl doesn't know the difference, and neither do my dinner guests.

Although the market offers many options, you do not need any special equipment for a good ice pop. With a handful of craft sticks (available at any art-supply shop), you can freeze ice pops in anything from paper cups to vintage baking tins. A plastic wrap–lined loaf pan is one of my favorite makeshift molds: pour in the mixture, cover tightly with a sheet of aluminum foil, and then insert the sticks through the foil in a row down the center at about 1-inch (2.5-cm) intervals. When frozen, lift from the pan and slice into ice pops.

Allow about 4 hours for most ice pops to freeze solid. Of course, the yield of these recipes depends on the size of your molds. The classic mold holds about 4½ tablespoons (2½ fl oz/ 75 ml). Here are three easy recipes; each one makes 8 to 12 ice pops, depending on the mold.

## chocolate pudding pops

1 cup (8 fl oz/250 ml) heavy cream

1¼ cups (10 fl oz/310 ml) whole milk

2 tablespoons unsweetened cocoa powder

1 teaspoon pure vanilla extract

Pinch of salt

4 oz (125 g) bittersweet or semisweet chocolate, chopped

1–3 tablespoons sugar

In a saucepan over medium heat, combine the cream, milk, cocoa powder, vanilla, and salt and bring to a simmer, whisking to dissolve the cocoa. Add the chocolate and stir until dissolved. Stir in the sugar to taste. Cool the mixture over an ice bath before freezing.

## coconut-cardamom ice pops

1 can (13½ fl oz/420 ml) coconut milk

½ cup (4 fl oz/125 ml) whole milk

¼ cup (1 oz/30 g) unsweetened shredded dried coconut

¼ teaspoon ground cardamom

⅛ teaspoon ground cinnamon

3 tablespoons dark rum (optional)

1–3 tablespoons maple syrup or honey

In a bowl, whisk together all the ingredients except the maple syrup until well blended. Whisk in the maple syrup to taste.

## watermelon mojito ice pops

⅓ cup (1½ oz/45 g) diced seedless watermelon

¼ cup (¼ oz/7 g) loosely packed fresh mint leaves, finely chopped

¼ cup (2 fl oz/60 ml) light rum

2 tablespoons fresh lime juice

1 tablespoon grated lime zest

2–3 teaspoons sugar

⅔ cup (5 fl oz/160 ml) club soda

In a blender, combine the watermelon, mint, rum, lime juice and zest, and 1 teaspoon sugar and process until smooth and the mint is reduced to flecks. Taste and adjust the sweetness if necessary. Stir in the club soda.

Biscotti are one of those treats you see in a glass jar on the counter in a café or in the display case in a bakery but may not consider making them at home. They're actually quite easy to make, and they store well. Biscotti are forgiving, too, since they are meant to be hard, inviting dips into coffee, tea, milk, or dessert wine.

# chocolate-cherry biscotti with almonds *makes about 2½ dozen*

½ cup (2½ oz/75 g) slivered blanched almonds

¾ cup (4½ oz/140 g) unsweetened dried cherries

3 tablespoons kirsch

2¾ cups (14 oz/440 g) unbleached all-purpose flour, plus more for dusting

¼ cup (¾ oz/20 g) unsweetened cocoa powder

1 teaspoon baking powder

⅛ teaspoon salt

3 large eggs

1 cup (8 oz/250 g) sugar

1 teaspoon pure almond extract

6 oz (185 g) semisweet chocolate, very finely chopped

Preheat the oven to 325°F (165°C). Line 2 baking sheets with parchment paper.

In a small, dry frying pan, toast the almonds over medium heat, stirring constantly, until fragrant and lightly browned, about 5 minutes. Pour onto a plate to cool. Set aside.

In a small bowl, combine the cherries and kirsch and toss to coat the cherries. Set aside.

In a medium bowl, whisk together the flour, cocoa powder, baking powder, and salt. In a large bowl, beat the eggs with the sugar and almond extract until well blended and lightened in color. Add the flour mixture and chocolate and beat until a dough forms. Drain the cherries. Scatter the cherries and almonds on top of the dough and fold in until evenly distributed.

Turn the dough out onto a lightly floured work surface and divide in half. Shape each portion into a flattish log about 3 inches (7.5 cm) wide, 8 inches (20 cm) long, and 1 inch (2.5 cm) thick. Arrange the 2 dough logs on 1 of the prepared baking sheets, leaving at least 1 inch (2.5 cm) of space around them on all sides.

Bake until firm to the touch, 25–30 minutes. Let cool on the pan on a wire rack until cool enough to handle, then transfer to a large cutting board. Using a large serrated knife, using a gentle sawing motion, cut the logs crosswise on a slight diagonal into slices about ½ inch (12 mm) wide.

Divide the biscotti between the 2 baking sheets, arranging them on a cut side. Return to the oven and bake for 10 minutes. Turn over the biscotti and continue to bake until dry to the touch, about 10 minutes longer. Let cool on the pans on wire racks. Store in an airtight container at room temperature for up to 1 month.

## fresh take

Here I use the classic combination of chocolate, almonds, and cherries—but other dried fruit and nut combinations are possible, too, such as dried currants and pine nuts, dried cherries and hazelnuts, or dried blueberries and walnuts.

## pack to go

Biscotti are a great dessert to bring to any dinner or party. For easy transport, wrap them in parchment paper and tie with string; stack them in a lunch box, placing a sheet of parchment between each layer; or stand them up in a tin or jar.

## perfect partner

Biscotti were made for dunking in *vin santo* but any sweet dessert wine pairs well.

# INDEX

# weldonowen

415 Jackson Street, Suite 200, San Francisco, CA 94111
Telephone: 415 291 0100  Fax: 415 291 8841
www.wopublishing.com

### GOOD FOOD TO SHARE

Conceived and produced by Weldon Owen, Inc.
In collaboration with Williams-Sonoma, Inc.
3250 Van Ness Avenue, San Francisco, CA 94109

### A WELDON OWEN PRODUCTION

Copyright © 2010 Weldon Owen, Inc. and Williams-Sonoma, Inc.
All rights reserved, including the right of reproduction
in whole or in part in any form.

Color separations by Embassy Graphics in Canada
Printed and bound by Toppan-Leefung in China

First printed in 2010
10 9 8 7 6 5 4 3 2 1

Library of Congress Cataloging-in-Publication
data is available.

ISBN-13: 978-1-61628-071-0
ISBN-10: 1-61628-071-9

Weldon Owen is a division of
**BONNIER**

### WILLIAMS-SONOMA, INC.

Founder and Vice-Chairman  Chuck Williams

### WELDON OWEN, INC.

CEO and President  Terry Newell
VP, Sales and Marketing  Amy Kaneko
Director of Finance  Mark Perrigo

VP and Publisher  Hannah Rahill
Associate Publisher  Amy Marr
Associate Editor  Julia Humes

Creative Director  Emma Boys
Designer  Lauren Charles

Production Director  Chris Hemesath
Production Manager  Michelle Duggan
Color Manager  Teri Bell

Photographer  Ray Kachatorian
Food Stylist  Valerie Aikman-Smith
Prop Stylists  Emily Henson and Leigh Noe

### ACKNOWLEDGMENTS

From Sara Kate Gillingham-Ryan: The Weldon Owen team astounds me with their great taste and efficiency. Hannah Rahill charmed and supported me from day one, and Amy Marr gave me hard deadlines and tall orders, but also wiggle room and friendship. I'm so glad we met. When I first saw the photographs for the book, I was stunned. Cookbook authors are not always so blessed with images they feel represent their kind of cooking, but this time around, I was lucky. The images on these pages were born from Ray Kachatorian's thoughtful and hungry eye, Valerie Aikman-Smith's effortless food styling, and Emily and Leigh's spot-on prop styling. Emma Boys brought it all together in a beautiful way and I thank her for it. My mother, Karen Gillingham, helps me in every aspect of my life from babysitting to recipe testing. Many of the recipes in this book have her touch. Maxwell and Ursula Gillingham-Ryan are my loving teammates and cheerleaders, night after night, bite after bite. They are usually patient and always hungry, so it's a good fit. There wasn't a single person on this project who didn't share my vision of why we gather around tables and share food, so I thank you all for putting your true selves into this work.

**Weldon Owen** wishes to thank the following people for their generous support in producing this book: Linda Bouchard, Keiko Brodeur, Conor Collins, Becky Duffett, Adam Dunn, Rebecca Farr, Rachel Goldman, Gregory Han, Emily Ho, Alexa Hyman, Chuck Luter, Carrie Neves, Jennifer Newens, Elizabeth Parson, Karen Seriguchi, Sharon Silva, and Lauren Stocker.

### PHOTOGRAPHY CREDITS
All photographs by Ray Kachatorian